CANDLE MAKING
BUSINESS MADE EASY

**A Step by Step Guide on How to Start, Run and Grow
a Home-Based Candle Making Business - Launch
Your Startup and Make Money Fast From Scratch**

Melissa Farrell

BONUS LIBER

Contents

Introduction

Hello, my name is Melissa, and I want to let you in on a bit of a secret. Ever since I can remember, I have always been a creative person. From crafting homemade decorations to going to art exhibitions, trying to understand the deep meanings behind paintings or sculptures, you name it, and I probably was into it. Furthermore, even though I don't cook on a daily basis, I am the kind of person who finds baking very relaxing and decorating cakes therapeutic.

In other words, I have always been good at working with my hands and had an inclination towards art. However, like most people of my generation, I was told that to succeed in life, you have to choose a safe path, a 9 to 5 job, and not some dreamy artistic existence. I was explicitly told that painting on the banks of Seine simply doesn't happen in real life. So instead of going to art school, I studied something *'practical,'* as my parents called it. After graduation, I took a desk career and let my abilities linger somewhere in the back.

Truth be told, in time, I learned to love my job. I was so busy at the office that I simply forgot about the bohemian dreams I had growing up, and my creativity started to fade a little each day. But I didn't mind. I loved my life, and I couldn't even imagine it other than what it was.

Well, the joke was on me.

If you haven't been living under a rock for the past two years, then you know about the pandemic, how it affected everybody, and so on. You definitely don't need to hear this part again. However, I will tell you my story and how this COVID-19 situation changed me and my life.

Like in so many cases, the company I was working for was forced to declare bankruptcy soon after the global lockdown, leaving me jobless in a non-hiring world.

So what do you do when you are in a no-money and no-job situation? You buy yourself a bottle of red wine, cry yourself to sleep, and think about possible solutions, right? No! I mean, yes, that's what I did, but you should not do it.

Anyway, long story short, the next day, with the bottle of wine empty on my countertop, I started to write down all my qualities. It was my only way of figuring out what to do with my life.

I might add that when you are low, your self-esteem is even lower, so thinking about your pluses is not an easy task.

Therefore, an hour and many tears later, the list only contained *patience* as my sole quality, so I decided to light up a scented candle. I mean, if you have to pity yourself, at least do it in a nice smelling room. Right?

But, as soon as my match touched the wick, it instantly hit me - I love crafting, and my state of misery was giving me all the time in the world to do it. For the first time since kindergarten, I was able to play with clay or whatever without anyone nagging me. I was allowed to do everything I wanted because I had no better things to work on.

So I ran to my laptop and checked out some tutorials. By the following morning, I had already ordered myself a *'make your own candle'* kit, and that was it. Each day I learned something new and improved my technique. In a couple of months, I had so many candles that I had to give some away. Receiving positive feedback from my friends reinforced me, offering me the confidence I needed to open my own candle business.

Today, after almost two years, I can honestly say that I never thought of myself as an entrepreneur. Still, I am so happy to have had the opportunity to let my creativity run free. The small business I now have gives me tons of satisfaction, economically and, most importantly, psychologically.

My self-esteem level today? Higher than the sky.

This being said, I decided to write this book as I am sure that many people today are wearing the shoes I had when COVID-19 shook my reality. This is the main reason why I want to share with you my collection of theoretical and practical knowledge on the matter with the hope that it will help you along the way.

Therefore, if you want to follow my path, I won't lie to you and say it will be easy because it won't. I won't tell you that there won't be days in which you'll want to quit. But I will tell you that success is yours to grab if you really want it. Also, I will tell you that delaying the start won't do you any good. You will just wake up more miserable than the day before.

Without further ado, are you ready to start this wonderful journey together? I bet you are, so let's begin!

CHAPTER ONE

A Burning Fascination

P eople always have - for some mysterious reason - been fascinated by flames.

Candles are the perfect example of a flame that makes us feel better, warmer and relaxed. During a candle's burning, it light and heat, and the flame appears to be writhing around the wick. One can't help but stare in awe at how and why the flame on the wick burns.

Watching a candlewick's flame burn can lead some people into contemplation and often into a dream-like state. It can inspire calm, induce meditation and sometimes arouse feelings of love and passion. For this reason, candlelight dinners are popular.

Before going into more detailed discussions, I want to tell you that I am not a person of many convictions. Yet, it is my firm belief that to appreciate and truly love your work, you need to understand how it got to be what it is today. It doesn't matter if we discuss crafting candles, jewelry, or even studying to become a doctor. To be good at your job, you need to respect your profession. And you can only do so by understanding its past.

And since I want you to enjoy reading this book, I will tell you a story. I will take you on a journey through time. Together, we will discover the history of candles and understand how they have transformed from objects of necessity into ones of relaxation.

Furthermore, I will tell you everything you need to know about these items before you consider starting a candle business.

The Fascinating History Of Candles

First of all, I want you to find a very comfortable position and try a mental exercise. Close your eyes and think for a minute. Can you guess when candles were invented? Was it throughout the Middle Ages, or are they older? Hmm? Do you have any ideas?

Truth be told, nobody knows exactly how life was more than 5000 years ago. Even ancient history doesn't go further in time than that. Historians say that history begins with the year 3000 BC, and what happened before that time is prehistory.

Why is that, you might ask? Well, simply because there are no written documents to guide us in reconstructing the past.

Yet, we know for a fact that even from the early 3000 BC, when the first pages of history were being drafted, candles were already part of humans' lives.

Of course, 5000 years ago, candles were not precisely what they are today. Even so, those ancient versions are still considered to be the support pillars of their whole existence and development.

It is debatable which civilization was the first to use candles. Still, records put the Egyptians and the Romans among the people who might have created the first prototype.

If I were to bet my money, I would bet it on the Egyptians. However, since I am far from being a historian, I will tell you both stories, and you can decide which tale seems more veridic.

So let's start with Ancient Egypt. It's impossible not to have heard of them. You know, pharaohs, Cleopatra, mummies, pyramids, and all that advanced technology that still no one understands completely. Therefore, it's no wonder they are in historians' viewfinder when it comes to this topic as well.

When archeologists discovered some unidentified bronze objects dating from the early 3000 BC in Egypt, they raised the interest of chroniclers and anthropologists. After studying them, scientists decided that these items were, in fact, some kind of candleholders.

Correlating these holders with other information, researchers concluded that Egyptians were soaking the reeds' pithy core in either tallow or melted animal fat. Furthermore, they used rolled papyrus or pieces of rush plants instead of actual wicks. And since these primitive candles were probably too soft, they needed the holders I was telling you about earlier.

Now, even though there is no physical discovery to support this theory, some historians claim that Romans could have invented candles long before Egyptians. Since this is clearly a debatable piece of information, I will tell you something that it's not.

The Romans were the ones who realized the necessity of making candles stronger and invented the notion of 'wick.' It was designed by rolling papyrus and melting it in beeswax. One of the reasons they needed these objects to be more resistant was their use in religious ceremonies, which lasted for longer periods of time.

But you know what? Egyptians and Romans weren't the only advanced civilizations that inhabited Earth at that time. No, there were others.

For instance, ancient Greeks are considered the first to use 'birthday candles.' They placed candles on top of round cakes and offered them to the Moon Goddess, Artemis. For them, the candlelight represented the moon, while the candle smoke was the means of transportation for their prayers up to the sky and Artemis.

On the other hand, the first time candles were mentioned in Asia's history was thousands of years later, more precisely during the Chinese Qin Dynasty (259-210 BC).

Actually, real candles dating from that time were recently found in the mausoleum of Qin Shi Huang, the first emperor of its Dynasty.

Furthermore, it is believed that Asian civilizations were the ones who added fragrances to their candles. For instance, they used nutty oils in Japan while the Indians added cinnamon fruits to enhance the candles' smell.

But, moving along in history with another 100 years or so, it is safe to say that the first civilization which really gave meaning to the importance of candles within religious ceremonies was the Jew one. Even today, after almost 2000 years, the Jewish communities all over the world celebrate Hanukkah in the same way they did the first time in 165 BC - they light candles for eight days and eight nights, turning the whole celebration into a festival of lights.

As populations expanded, so did the need for a lighting form. Thus, naturally, when the Middle Ages came knocking, people's life depended on candles. And that is why the Medieval era represents a very big moment for the candle industry.

By the 13th century, a new profession was born. People all over the European continent but especially in France and England started making and selling candles in special shops. Moreover, these candlemakers, known as chandlers, were going door to door, collecting kitchen fat from the locals, fat which they then crafted into candles. So, at that time, in Europe, candles were strictly made out of animal fat, more precisely tallow.

However, as society grew, so did the wealthy people's demands. And the tallow-made candles had a huge problem - they were highly smokey.

In response to the upper class' needs, candle manufacturers started using beeswax for the first time in Europe. The improvement was indeed remarkable as these candles burn without producing smoke, leaving behind a fresh and pleasant fragrance.

Unfortunately, since they were more expensive to manufacture, these items were solely used by the church for its religious ceremonies and by the rich population who could afford to buy them for personal benefit.

Anyway, hundreds of years later, during colonial time, thanks to the women in America, the production of candles took a new turn. To create clean yet aromatic, sweet-smelling wax, these inventive ladies boiled grayish-green berries of the bayberry bushes. However, extracting the resin from these bushes was not an easy task, making the popularity of bayberry candles decrease.

But the 18th century came, and with it, so did the big industrial revolution. As you probably guessed, the candle-making process was not left behind and was influenced by industrialization.

During this period, the significant change was marked by a wax called *'spermaceti,* ' obtained by crystallizing sperm whale oil. The reasons why spermaceti candles became so popular are multiple. For one, they burned with a clear, bright light without generating unpleasant smoke. Furthermore, in addition to beeswax, spermaceti candles were stronger, and they burned for more hours.

But for the candle industry, the most significant impact was not during the famous industrial revolution. No. For the candle-making sector, the most important moment happened in the 19th century, and the man who changed everything was Michel Eugene Chevreul. He discovered a way to extract stearic acid from fatty acids, creating a very durable candle material, allowing them to burn for many hours with a clean burn.

Even so, it was only after the invention of Joseph Morgan that the candle industry truly thrived. What he did was automate the process of manufacturing. The series production of candles made them less expensive and, therefore, more affordable for everyone.

The final progress came in 1850 when scientists separated a natural waxy-like substance from petroleum, producing what we now know as paraffin. Very soon, they realized that this newly discovered wax was actually perfect for being used as raw material for making candles.

Paraffin candles were a game-changer. They burned with a clean and odorless flame, but most importantly, they were cheap.

However, by the end of the 19th century, the demand for candles decreased due to the magic of electricity. And once again, candles entered a new era.

After 50 years or so in which people considered candles simply overrated, the US oil industry bloomed, taking along byproducts such as paraffin and stearic acid compounds.

Therefore, by the early 90s, candles of all different shapes, colors, and sizes were available in almost any market. They were seen as a trendy decorative piece, and therefore candles were considered the perfect item to be gifted.

Now, even though the last decade of the 20th century is not necessarily known as one of the most important for science and technology, it actually meant a lot for the candle industry. After more than a century, researchers announced that they discovered two more resins suitable for crafting candles - soybean wax and palm wax.

However, in the last 20 years, nothing really worth mentioning has happened. That's why I want to fast-forward you a little until present times.

It is true that today, candles don't represent a necessity anymore. Yet, their popularity grows by the day, making the candle industry worth around 3 billion dollars.

But that's not all. Since wax supplies are very affordable nowadays, it opened a great door for home crafters like myself to turn their passion into a real business.

The Science Behind The Perfect Flame

I am almost sure that you didn't expect to learn so much about candles' history when you first started this book. Well, neither did I when I really began to study the matter. But with each page I read, I became more and more fascinated with candles. That's why I wanted to share this information with you because I do hope you'll feel the same way.

There are many details I skipped because, in the end, this is a guide on how to start a business and not a history book. Yet, you now know how candles started from early antiquity before turning into the lovely decorative objects they are today.

But how do they work? I mean, clearly, you light them, and they burn. But how? Is there something that you should know before crafting candles?

Well, yes, but the process is extremely easy to understand. From the first time you light up a candle, you start a series of combustion reactions. In other words, candles burn using the same principle as old-school incandescent lamps - they both generate light due to heat production.

All this is possible thanks to the wax's response to oxygen when heated. The final result? A very common colorless gas we know as carbon dioxide, but also heat, steam, and, of course, light.

By producing heat, the wax is melted, releasing enough fuel for the combustion reaction.

To paint a more visual image, you should know that the candle's flame reaches really high temperatures, which is why it has the power to start the ignition process. I am talking about temperatures between 1800 and 2550 Fahrenheit. That is around the same degrees lava has when running the Earth's surface.

Anyway, the whole burning and releasing heat process is under a continuous loop that breaks only when the wick burns down or there is no more wax left.

However, as simple as it is, I will be honest with you and tell you that sometimes, things don't go as planned. Truth be told, everything needs to be in a complete balance for your candle to burn clean and constant. This is why you may find that lighting a candle for the first time doesn't go as perfectly as you'd expect. It actually might take a while for the combustion reaction to reach a steady state and remain stable.

The same explanation applies to candles that burn with a flickering flame even after more than one use. In these cases, very often, the problem is the wick. It is probably not correctly trimmed, and therefore the flame can't find a stable spot to burn clear in its teardrop shape. However, if you clip your wick constantly and correctly, you should not encounter any problems.

But since the chemical outcome is different based on the compounds implicated in the reaction, you should expect each candle to be somehow unique when it comes to its burning process. This is a more complex discussion, and we should not diminish its importance. That is why I will return to this part when we talk more in-depth about wax and wick types.

But until then, let's talk about business!

CHAPTER TWO

Why to Start Your Own Candle Business

R emember how I told you that today's candle industry is estimated to be around 3 billion dollars? I wasn't lying. Moreover, in less than four years, specialists predict that this sector's worth will almost double, reaching the impressive amount of 5 billion dollars.

As you can imagine, this is not just thanks to your average Jane, Mary, or any other typical woman who is interested in accessorizing her home. No. The boost of candles' commercial use is directly linked to the increased interest people recently started to show in massage and spa therapies. But that's not all. The candle industry is also extremely supported by worldwide restaurants that try to create a romantic atmosphere for their clients by placing a small candle on their tables.

Even though many of these, let's call them service providers as I can't think of a better name to include spas, restaurants, and hotels, don't spend too much when purchasing their candles, you will discover that there are cases in which they look for quality and not quantity. And as a manual crafter, you can provide excellent quality.

Yet you should understand that once you start a candle business, you can address anyone interested in buying your products. Yes, candles are usually sold in home department stores, gift shops, or supermarkets. But, I need you to understand that when it comes to finding your market, the sky's the limit, and don't let anyone tell you otherwise. Especially, don't listen to advice from people who don't know how this domain works because they are probably wrong and can only take you down.

To help you understand the significance behind my words, I will share a story from when I started my company. I was at the point where I almost had everything I needed for my business to be up and running. The only thing I was waiting for was the legal documents to be approved. So, I was in a supermarket, checking out some candles to see what type of package they use, their fragrances, and so on. I already had a few molds and fragrance recipes which I tested and was very pleased with. Nevertheless, I wanted to find inspiration to do more. And there is no better way to succeed than knowing your competition.

Anyway, I was minding my own business when an acquaintance noticed me and came to say hello. One thing led to another, and I told her how I was starting my own company. Basically, I explained to her everything that had happened to me in the last months. Even now, after so much time, I can still hear her exact words, "*Why in the world would you start a candle business in the middle of the summer? Why don't you find something else to do and maybe get back to this idea around Christmas when people actually buy candles?"*

Imagine how devastated I was when I left that supermarket. I had all my hopes and dreams, not to mention all my money, put in this business. And in less than 5 minutes, one woman, who I am sure had all the best intentions, made me doubt everything.

Luckily for me, I didn't have any other choice than to go further. So very soon, I learned that there were other aspects I had to figure out. There were marketing angles I had no idea how to address. I had to find an accountant because paperwork is not an easy walk-in-the-park. I had to find proper storage for the hard-to-sell candles, because yes, you will have some not-so-popular models. Therefore, being in the wrong season was the least of my problems. Actually, I quickly discovered that the candles sold during the holiday season represent only around 30% of the total sales you make in a year.

In any case, my point is simple - only follow the advice backed by data. The rest are just opinions, and you will have to bear plenty of them, no doubt about it.

To draft an idea on what to expect, try to count how many people you know, and that is the rough number of theories you will be receiving. The only suggestion I can make in this case is to try and filter them so they won't take your morals down. If you don't know how to do so, just write the pros and cons of each idea you have. This way, when a person tells you to reconsider your approach, you will take a data-driven decision and not an emotional one.

For instance, let me help you start this list with the most complex and important topic - why start a candle-making business. Because, in the end, that's the part you should begin with. And from personal experience, I can assure you that it's not an easy task. Therefore, to assist you on the matter, I will share my own notes to which you can add your own bullet points.

Pros

As you've seen, I decided to become an entrepreneur and have a word to say in the candle business world due to circumstances out of my control.

However, my main pro reason for adventuring into this domain was **having the possibility of doing something I truly loved**.

Because this is a fact - getting into crafting candles allows people to make use of their passions. It lets them devote their time and energy to ensure their business' success.

In other words, if you choose to start your own candle-crafting company, you will most definitely feel as if you are practicing your hobby over and over again. You won't feel the chore of having to work each day, and you won't feel the frustration of working on something that you don't like just for the sake of money.

Furthermore, this should go without saying, but **you will be your own boss**. All the decisions you make will be your own. You will decide when to work and how much you work. Simply put, you will call all the shots, and trust me, that will empower you. Because I don't know the background you come from, but for me, not having to go to daily stand-ups and meet-ups simply felt liberating.

Another plus that not many jobs can offer you is incredible **flexibility**. You can work from literally anywhere. You can work from home, rent a studio or travel the world selling your candles in local markets or fairs. Yes, you can even live a fascinating nomad life and have a different kind of fun each day.

But, speaking of selling your candles, it is safe to say that probably you will start with an online approach as it is the most comfortable one, to begin with. Why? Basically, having an online business has more than one perk. Let's face it, **eCommerce** is the new way of shopping, and it's here to stay. Not only can you build your own website and grow your traffic, but you can also make use of other platforms. For instance, you can promote and sell your merchandise using **Amazon**, which is the largest online retailer, but you can also use **Facebook** or **Instagram Market**.

Simply put, you can **scale** your business as much as you want. You can add and remove features daily, implementing different approaches that will allow you to reach new customers.

A significant advantage that you should definitely consider since let's face it, everybody wants to make a profit is represented by the **high margins**. When we talk about making candles, we talk about an approximation of 35% gross margin, which is considerably high. Having such an excellent gross margin is very beneficial as it allows you to reinvest and grow your business.

Of course, since you are the decision-maker, you can raise your margin or **apply discounts** at any time. This way, you can help your clients decide, encouraging them to buy on impulse and enjoy the best promotional value.

Finally, you can build a community around your brand and benefit from their **referrals.**

Cons

Now, as you can imagine, just like in any other business, opening a candle-making company is not all rainbows and butterflies. There are also negative aspects, and you should be aware of them right from the start.

Ignoring the not-so-pretty parts will only make them bite you sooner or later. So, here are the situations that I believe to be vital to consider before launching yourself into this type of business.

First of all, there are many **legal aspects** you have to know. You will have to pay annual taxes regardless of how much you sell, and this can be a very big issue if you don't have enough profit or you don't save money for these taxes.

Furthermore, other expenses may occur. For example, you will probably have to **pay extra taxes** for selling your merchandise in other states.

The last thing you want is to have problems with the IRS. So, study very well the legislation for opening a business in your country or state and follow it to the letter.

I told you earlier that having high margins is a very big plus for me. However, in order to afford this luxury, you will need to **find good suppliers**. And let's just say that it can be a tricky thing to do. Why? Because you want good quality raw materials, reasonable prices, discounts, and reliability. So, yeah, good suppliers don't grow in every tree.

Anyway, even after figuring out all the legal aspects and finding your perfect vendor, you will still have difficulties.

As I said, this is a $ 3 billion industry so, don't expect the **competition** to be anything but harsh. You have to understand what they are doing so you can do better or cheaper, depending on the clients you wish to target.

Since you will compete with hundreds if not thousands of candle businesses, you will need to convince people to choose you from the crowd. And **building trust** is difficult to accomplish, especially if you focus only on the online presence. People like online shopping, but they usually buy products they already know. They buy products for which they don't need a face-to-face interaction to make a decision.

When you market your products online, there are many benefits, but unfortunately, taking that extra mile to get customers is not the only problem.

For example, you will have to be really careful with the data provided by your clients. You will thoroughly have to **build security measures** not to leak it. This is a very delicate matter that should not be bypassed. Furthermore, if you decide to go globally, you must be extremely careful about selling your products in Europe. They have additional policies regarding data protection, so to sell within the European Union, you will have to be GDPR compliant.

Now, I don't know if this is a minus for everyone, but I am a social animal, so I struggled not to get depressed when I started my company. Since you will be working on your own, you may feel the **isolation** pressure.

This can be an even bigger issue during times in which sales don't go as you wish. Because there are **good days and bad days,** and on the days in which no one even visits your website, not to mention making a purchase, being alone in your house can be a little bit overwhelming.

And finally, be prepared for **receiving hate**. Not everybody is going to love you. There will be people that haven't even bought anything from you but will still leave you mean comments. I don't know why, but apparently, it's in human nature to rub dirt on others for no obvious reason.

Anyway, I told you that the road to success won't be easy. I warned you about this fact from the very beginning. You knew it, so there is no sense for you to back down now that you have realized the obstacles.

It's natural to be afraid, especially if you haven't got any entrepreneurship background.

In the end, this is why you are reading this book. You are reading it because you have a dream but don't know the steps to take and make it happen. You are reading it because I was where you are today; thus, I have many of the answers you are looking for.

That's why I want you to find yourself a piece of paper and a pen. The introduction part is over, and it's time to tackle the real aspects of getting your business up and running.

So let me hear you! Are you with me?

CHAPTER THREE

Easy Steps to Create Your Business Plan

U p until now, we basically just got to know each other. In other words, you only started to scratch the surface in understanding the steps to take to create a candle-making business and be a successful entrepreneur. Because there's no point in starting a company, investing your time and money if you don't profit from it. Without constant earnings, it is simply not worth it. Without stable revenues, you should keep your crafting as a hobby and find a job to support yourself.

So to succeed, the first piece of advice I can give you is to be serious about the whole deal. Don't even think about jumping on that train without getting your ducks in a row.

The better you organize right from the beginning, the easier it will be for you later.

My proposal to you is this. Let's take each relevant step at a time. I want to explicitly describe each phase so you can really understand everything. My only request is to take your time when reading this chapter. Don't rush it. If you feel like taking a break, close the book and take that break.

It will be a long and vital chapter, so the last thing you want is to hurry yourself up and don't accumulate the information. Because what you are about to read next is what makes the difference between success and failure.

So once again, let me start by telling you my story.

Have At Least One Perfect Craft

When I decided to launch my company, I couldn't even imagine doing so without having at least one perfect prototype. God only knows how many times my friends told me I had a great product, and I still felt like I had to improve it.

However, as I talked to fellow candle crafters, I discovered that not everybody was as crazily thorough as me. As a matter of fact, I had the opportunity to meet some ladies who, in their opinion, did everything by the book but failed miserably. When we got to talking, I very soon found out that they had some kind of recipe from which they started, but they were not consistent. They used whatever raw materials were on discount, they didn't necessarily respect proportions, and so on. Naturally, they managed to sell some of their candles in fairs and flea markets, but they never managed to retain customers.

They were shocked when I suggested that maybe their inconsistency is the main reason for their problems. *"But we are crafters,"* they said, *"Crafted goods are not as commercial series ones. They are meant to be unique."*

At this point, I realized that they were as correct as I was. Crafted products need to be authentic. They need to let the customers know that they were manually produced, that someone thought about each ingredient used for its manufacture.

However, clients want consistency even when buying home-made products. Think about the homemade hot sauce for a second. How would it be to buy three bottles of the same hot sauce and each of them to have a different spicy level? I am sure that you wouldn't like that.

The same applies to candles and the clients buying them. They want the same fragrance level when they light their candles. They want the same colors, and they want the same melting point. They don't want to buy the vanilla candle they loved the last time they purchased it and discover that it barely leaves any odor.

Therefore, the first thing you need to do before even thinking of founding a company is to create at least one ideal recipe.

And I hate to be the one to break it for you, but if you don't have enough experience, you won't be able to create the perfect craft. Because yes, candles are complex to manufacture, more complicated than people think. It's not just melting wax and mixing it with some oils. No. There is a learning curve that no one can teach you if you don't practice your brains out.

Of course, I will tell you everything about wax types, wicks, molds, colors, and fragrances. I will explain how each one works, but if you don't exercise day after day after day, you won't excel. Even worse, you can create a product that could endanger you or your clients. Remember that you are literally playing with fire.

Anyway, and you can call me old-fashioned, but my suggestion is to write down the steps you take each day. This will allow you to understand your mistakes and also remember the successes.

Another thing that I want to highlight is that when you try to create your first fragrances, don't go too sweet or too floral from the start. Create a mild version and begin from there. Find some honest friends to help with their reviews.

However, the candle's smell is not the only thing you will have to learn how to replicate. You will have to discover on your own how to ensure a good burn time and which wax suits your style and approach.

Don't try to copy what others do. This will not make you stand out from the crowd. Find something unique to add to your candles. You can find inspiration anywhere. Think of what you love and add it to your work.

For instance, I find a smell, a taste, or a color on each holiday I take. I then try to add it into a new candle and see how it goes. Anyway, this is just an example, and you should figure out what inspires you and what makes you special.

When you'll finally discover the correct recipe, repeat it a couple of times and give your friends candles from various batches to see if they can't figure out the differences. Repeat the process until not even you can spot the distinctions between two candles.

After you master a recipe from top to bottom, only then can you consider yourself ready for the next entrepreneurship journey.

Write Down Your Business Plan

After you make sure that you are talented enough and your candles are ready to compete in this harsh world, it's time to make an attack plan. Well, in this case, the attack is a metaphorical way of saying you will draft the blueprint of your business.

And since most often than not, creative people don't really like to write down affair approaches, well, you might not like this part too much.

My advice to you is to look at it like any other project. Think about it as if writing down the instructions on crafting the perfect candle.

Yes, it's a little bit more analytical, but it will be good for you. I can assure you that after a couple of hours of looking at numbers and figuring out paths, you will be dying to try out some new oils and waxes, making your creativity bloom.

Anyway, a well-written business plan has the purpose of guiding you along the way, helping you to grow your organization in a healthy organic manner. Furthermore, a well-written plan can also help you get a loan. It even has the power to attract possible investors.

Writing such a scheme from scratch seems impossible if you are new to the game. Luckily, the internet is full of templates and software to help you.

However, before anything else you'll need to focus on just a few aspects, and I will explain them to you. After that, you can choose a template and put down your visions.

Find Your Market Target

So you already have that perfect candle or candles you want to start your business with. But who will you address? Did you think about what kind of clients you will attract?

Going in blindly without knowing your target market is not the best approach.

The candle-making industry is versatile, and therefore there are many business approaches to take. It really depends on which one suits your style and your visions.

Think about the products you make or wish to start making. Are they premium candles, or are they cheap? Are they suitable for elegant, sumptuous spaces or for cozy cottages? Are they natural flavored or not?

You really need to decide and create products that people in that category look for.

The good thing about selling candles is that it is not influenced by your customers' ethnicity or educational level. But it is influenced by people's preference regarding fragrances, and regarding their green nature. Of course, it's also influenced by the purchasing power of your clients. Now, some might tell you that it's a gender-biased business. Again, that is the exact misconception I was telling you about earlier, the advice you should not listen to. Yes, women buy more candles than men, but men love candles just as much.

Anyway, there are a few categories of candle buyers, and you should decide which one you want to target with your products. This will help you very much when building your brand and marketing strategy, which we will talk about later. Furthermore, it will help you choose your suppliers and raw materials. In other words, knowing your target market will help show you the roads to pick along the way.

But for now, let's understand the three main client typologies with each pro and cons.

The lowest quality candles address the **mass market**. These candles are affordable and easy to craft, especially for beginners. It's no shame to start with these types of candles as they will help you learn and improve your techniques. Furthermore, once you manage to retain customers, they will bring you a nice profit.

However, there are, of course, some downsides when it comes to this category. First of all, the competition is intense. Not only will you compete with home crafters, but you will also go back to back with commercial brands that have been on the market for a long time and have teams of marketers on their payroll.

Another thing to consider is that it will be very difficult to expand selling your products beyond flea markets and maybe some small gift shops. Once people categorize you as being a cheap brand, it will be challenging to reach a more sophisticated public.

The next target market in line is the **mid-market** one. If you want to position yourself to attract customers that usually buy their candles from retail stores such as Target, Ikea, or Home Depot, be prepared as you will be competing with giant brands.

In my opinion, this category is the most difficult one to target. These people don't necessarily look for quality but for well-known brands. They don't have a problem spending $10-15 on a candle if it's bought from a store they like and trust.

So, even though it might seem a better idea to go with mid-range priced candles, I honestly think that you won't have an easy life with this approach.

Finally, suppose you really are a good crafter and are serious about your work. In that case, you should try to penetrate the **high-end market** category.

Truth be told, the demand for luxury candles has grown tremendously in the last few years. These products are manufactured using only high-premium natural raw materials.

Furthermore, their packaging needs to stand out and denote opulence.

Clients within this market target seek crafted candles and don't have a problem spending even $100 per candle. Yes, you read it correctly. With the right brand and quality, you can charge as much. After all, Louis Vuitton sells $185 candles.

Now, the disadvantage of this category is that you are not allowed to make any mistakes. Each candle you sell needs to be perfect in any sense.

I will return to the market targets when we'll talk about raw materials, but you get the point - depending on what and are capable of crafting, you will fit in a precise category. Therefore, let's move on.

After you decide on your target market, you can make other decisions such as selling only series candles or making them individualized based on your client's wishes. Even though the latter is quite hard to achieve, especially at the beginning, you may attract many clients who seek originality and want products created just for them.

Anyway, with a target market in mind and a prototype in your hand, you have to move forward. In other words, you need to establish your business identity. Thus, you need to create your brand.

Create a Brand

Branding is crucial for your success, so you have to get it right. And since I imagine that you won't hire a company to aid you in creating an attractive identity for your candle-making business, well, you will have to learn to master this part.

If you wonder if branding is truly worth the effort, stop it. There is no point in losing time with thoughts leading in that direction. And no, just finding a name for your business is not enough.

Imagine seeing an ID card that has only a name on it. Imagine looking at a piece of paper with just the name written there, no photo of who that person is, and no data about them. How do you know if they are real or scammers? The same thing happens with companies that fail to understand the importance of branding.

Your brand is the absolute representation of who you are as a business. It's your reputation as well as your responsibility.

If branding wouldn't be so important, do you think that giant companies such as Coca-Cola would invest around 400 million dollars each year in keeping their image popular? I guess not.

Anyway, the process of branding is not just a one-time thing, but a continuous operation that never stops. Once you are on the market, you have to adapt to its needs. You have to evolve and reinvent yourself in order to keep pace with the trends. Markets change, and so do the consumers. The latest in fashion today is the old news of tomorrow.

So, you have to create an easily shiftable and versatile brand.

Remember how I told you about possible investors? Yes, a candle-oriented company can attract business angels and stakeholders. Still, in a world in which almost 2000 startups are launched daily (and that is only in the US), investors tend to go with brands they can trust to be successful.

Simply put, you want to properly brand your company right from the start. It will open the door to new opportunities and increase your overall value.

Did I catch your attention? I bet I did.

As pompous as it all sounds, I can tell you that if you really believe in your product, no one will do a better job than you in branding it. And I will tell you exactly why that is.

First of all, no one knows your concept better than you; therefore, no one can understand your vision and put it into practice.

So, don't be scared. You got this under control. You are the king and queen of your ideas.

Therefore, let's move on!

For me, one of the excruciating parts was **choosing my business name.** I know that for some, this comes naturally, and I hope you are one of those people, but for me, figuring out a catchy name that I also liked was not an easy job.

In the end, my brainstorming took a more unorthodox approach, one that I will gladly share with you.

Now, if you look at any tutorial on how to name your business, they will all tell you that you have to come up with a memorable name. My first thought when I got this advice? "*No shit, Sherlock! I could have figured that out myself.*"

Yes, that's right. Finding a name for your company is easier said than done, especially in the era we live in when technically all the good names are already taken.

Anyway, I did what I read and tried to find a name that described my business, one that was easy to remember and, of course, sounded kind of cool. After many hours I was the proud *'mother'* of the name *'candling.'* I even had a motto - *"Candling all your problems away."*

Now imagine my disappointment when I Googled the name to see if it's available only to discover that *candling* is actually a word and it doesn't mean what I wanted it to mean. It represents a method used in embryology to study the growth and development of an embryo inside an egg.

Yeah. Laugh away and call me ignorant. But I am a big city gal, so raising chickens is not my area of interest.

Anyway, what I am trying to say is this. Don't focus on finding names strictly related to the word *'candle.'* You will just waste time and get frustrated.

Think of things you like, of things that have importance to you, and explore that angle. Don't worry if there is nothing good in this section. You have more options.

For instance, let's say that your main product is made with beeswax and has a lemony fragrance. Go simple with the name and call it *'H & L Candles'* as in *'honey and lemon.'* From there, you can play and reinvent yourself. But people will know that your trademark is that specific type of candle.

Another approach in finding a suitable business alias is to use your own name. I mean, all the big fashion houses do it, so why wouldn't you do the same? You might probably say you have a boring common name, but you are wrong. Think a little. Who was Coco before Chanel? She was just a girl with a name that means *"dweller near the canal."*

So is your surname something like Jackson? So what? Brand your business name as *"Jackie's Lights."*

In any case, I am sure that you got the point which is not to get stuck in finding the perfect name starting just with the word *'candle.'*

With your name problem all figured out, it's time to see if someone else didn't already think of it before you. So check to see if the web domain is available. Use platforms such as GoDaddy and check the availability. Of course, social media platforms are also very important. Investigate all possible places to make sure that you are free to use the business identity you want. If you are lucky enough to nail from the first try, buy the domain name and create the social media pages right away. You don't need to use them immediately, but it's good to reserve them for when you are ready to get started. Delaying this part can only turn into a bad surprise, and you could discover that in just a matter of hours, someone else took your brand's name.

The Legal Aspects

The next decision you will have to take is regarding the **legal structure** you prefer. If you live in the US, the most common ones to choose from are corporations, limited liability companies (LLCs), general partnerships, and sole proprietorships.

Depending on the type of business identity you'll choose, you will pay different taxes and have different benefits.

Unfortunately, I cannot really advise you which direction to take because I am not an expert on the matter. Therefore, I will tell you how I managed to decide.

Basically, I did what every person who is out of their comfort zone does - I hired a business attorney and asked for his opinion. You may think that it's too expensive to do so, but let me tell you that it was worth every penny. I would have probably lost more money paying taxes I didn't know about or fines for mistakes I wasn't even aware of.

Regardless of which type of organization you decide to open, you will need to register it to all the necessary federal and state agencies after choosing the business entity. I can't tell you if the procedures are the same in all states, and that's why I want to highlight the benefits of talking to an expert on the matter once more.

Anyhow, let's say that you figured things out and you have legally registered your business. Now what? Now you will have to **open a separate bank account** for your income.

You might be able to use your personal one if your company is a sole proprietorship. I don't know. However, I suggest you keep things separate as it will make your life so much easier when you have to pay your annual taxes. Furthermore, you need to also take into consideration not-so-happy endings. And in case of any lawsuits or even bankruptcy, your personal assets will be protected.

The bottom line is that you should open a separate bank account for everybody's sake.

At this point, legal advice would be once again very appreciated. My attorney was the one who recommended that I open separate accounts. Doing so, I make sure that I never spend the tax money on supplies and vice versa. It gives me an extra layer of protection because I am not the best when it comes to money predictions and things like that. I know that I have to put 25% of the income in a tax account and that I don't have to touch that money for any other reason than what they are meant for, which is paying my annual taxes.

As Benjamin Franklin said, "*In this world, nothing is certain except death and taxes.*"

Anyway, I find that having more accounts is really helpful for **tracking expenses**. Because yes, in order to have a solid business and sleep carefree at night, your bookkeeping needs to be impeccable. If your company will grow, in time, you will also need to hire an accountant. However, at first, you will be the one to keep track of everything.

Taking really good care of your bookkeeping will, of course, keep you safe from IRS audits, but it also helps you monitor your growth and allow you to make deductible expenses.

There are online services that can help you keep your records straight and organize your receipts. Now, it is true that the IRS only requires you to keep receipts for expenses higher than $75. Yet, I keep them all. You never know what might happen, and it's better to have your back covered.

The good thing about starting a candle-making business is that you will probably work from home, at least in the first months. This allows you to deduct the part of your house that you use as a studio, your internet, or your phone. If you personally go and buy the supplies, you can even deduct your transportation money.

However, keep in mind that any object that is used for both your personal and business life needs to be well described. For example, if you deduct your car's gas, you will need to present documentation that attests to your business miles. If you don't have papers that say exactly where you went and the purpose of your business trip, it won't be deductible.

Now, the bad news is that as an entrepreneur, you will have to learn many legal aspects. For instance, I had no idea that bookkeeping and accounting are different things. I was sure that once I could afford it, I would hire an accountant, forget about all the paperwork and focus only on the part I love, which is inventing new candles.

Yeah, that's as possible as visiting Peter Pan's Neverland.

Therefore, let me be the one to explain what you should expect.

Bookkeeping & Accounting

So, bookkeeping refers to the daily processes of recording your business' transactions, categorizing them, and so on. All this lies within your responsibilities as the manager of your company, and having an accountant won't change that.

On the other hand, accounting is a more complicated process that builds financial statements based on bookkeeping. I hope that makes sense because I don't really know how to explain it in more specialized terms since I am no expert in paperwork. Furthermore, each state has its own regulations, so you better read everything required for your location. Better yet, take my advice and talk to a tax expert.

Now, another aspect you should be aware of is that there are **two distinctive accounting methods** you will have to decide on. There is a cash method and an accrual one. I will take each one of these procedures and describe them as best as possible. So, the cash method recognizes the revenues and expenses when they are paid or received. On the other hand, the accrual method perceives them when they occur and requires the following receivables and payables. The thing you need to know about the accrual method is that it recognizes the transactions even if the payment isn't received by the bank yet.

Basically, when you are at the beginning of the road, you can choose which approach to go. However, you should know that US laws allow you to only use a cash accounting method if your revenues are below $5 million. If you exceed this amount, you will be legally obliged to move to the accrual method.

And that brings us to the next problem, which is **accepting payments**. Since you will probably be an online business, you will have to decide if you will be accepting credit cards or just debit cards. If you use a platform like Shopify to conduct your business, you won't have a problem with both card types. Shopify Payments facilitate everything you need for a smooth transaction.

However, if you want to be on your own, you will have to set up a merchant account. And this opens once more the discussion of having more than one bank account.

So, a merchant account is a financial account that allows you to accept credit card payments.

Another decision you have to make is you want to use third-party payment processors such as PayPal or Stripe. They can help you out to receive payments, but they will charge you for it. Depending on the processor you choose, the fees will differ.

You might think that going simple is the best way to start. However, I lost many possible clients simply because I didn't offer them the possibility of paying by PayPal. Therefore, yes, there are many aspects you need to consider before making a decision in this direction.

And since we are at the selling part, I think that it's only natural to talk about the **gross margin**. Remember how I told you that one of the benefits of having a candle-making business is its high gross margin? That's definitely true. However, you will need to learn how to calculate it.

But to do any of this, you first need to familiarize yourself with another term - the cost of goods sold (COGD). These are direct costs you have to produce your candles. Remember that you should not only add the materials when calculating the cost of goods sold. The labor is just as important.

All clear so far? Good!

Now, let's return to the gross margin. The gross margin symbolizes the profit left after subtracting the cost of producing the product, in your case, the candle.

Therefore, in order to calculate it, you will need to use a very simple mathematical formula.

Gross margin (%) = (revenue - COGS) / revenue

So the idea is simple. You can put as high a gross margin as you wish as long as the clients are okay with paying you that price.

The secret of managing to make a good profit without affecting your customer's pockets, making them feel cheated, is to find suppliers that sell you good raw materials but with noticeable discounts. That discount goes straight to your pocket as profit.

Unfortunately, since this is not always possible, you will have to learn how to juggle your candles' prices in such a way to attract customers but also to your benefit.

Now, unfortunately, not all the money you get from selling your candles belongs to you. No. Some of them need to go to the state in the form of taxes. However, others will be used to pay other people implicated in your business. You may think that you will be the only one involved in your company, but trust me, you don't want to keep it this way.

Playing a one-man show for too long, won't bring you the success you are looking for. So even though you will be alone in the first stages of your organization, you need to be prepared for when you will need to set up a proper payroll system.

There is more than one way in which you can procure outside help. For instance, you can classically hire yourself an employee or you can sign a contract with an independent freelancer. The outcome of the work they do for you should be more or less the same. However, when it comes to paying for their services, the situation becomes a little more complicated.

Let's take each of the situations separately so I can properly explain to you how things work.

Hiring someone to help you with different tasks might sound the best solution as it is the most traditional, but there are many implications to consider and not only payment ones.

The first thing you need to do is to apply for an EIN. Don't know what that means? Well, neither did I. So don't worry about it. Anyway, EIN stands for Employee Identification Number, which is a federal ID for businesses. You can apply for it directly on the IRS website. However, be prepared to offer details such as your social security number, corporation status or taxpayer ID.

But that's more. The next step you will have to take is to register with your state's unemployment insurance office. The reason why you have to take this step is because the US Department of Labor states that companies have to pay federal and state unemployment fees when employing at least one individual for 20 weeks in a year. Simply put you will have to register first with the state office in charge of unemployment insurance. After doing so, you will have to document your employees' quarterly salaries and pay the unemployment taxes online.

But let's move on away from the taxes for a second. Running background checks on your future employees is optional. You can ask for references and so on, but it's really up to you. However, it is mandatory to verify their identity using the U.S. Citizenship and Immigration Services' I-9 form.

With this out of the way, you will have to handle the employee's compensation insurance. As far as I know, some states don't request this step but make sure to check before skipping it as it is a vital part. This insurance will help you pay for medical costs in case your employee gets injured.

Another aspect that you need to take care of is to set up a payroll and tax withholding system for your employees. This includes Medicare and Social Security taxes. You will need to take care of W-4 forms and take into account the Fair Labor Standards Act. Basically, you will need to comply with all OSHA rules, which you can easily find on their website.

The only advice I can give you here is to make sure you have everything figured out before you hire someone.

Pff. That's it! We are done talking about accounting. So take a deep breath, drink a glass of water and take another comfortable seat as we ain't done speaking about legal aspects.

The next thing is optional. I had to do it because, as you know, I was jobless and more or less moneyless, but if you have some savings to get you started, you won't need the following hustle.

But if you are like me and can't afford to buy all the materials you need to start a business, you can ask for a **business credit card**. This is a way to secure your future funding. Now, depending on the bank you will choose, you will have to provide different documents, and you will have to pay various fees. But, regardless of the bank, you should expect the fees to be considerably higher than the ones you pay for your personal banking. Unfortunately, it is what it is, and we can't do anything about it.

Anyway, this mostly sums up everything you need to know in order to create a legitimate startup. I know that legal work is no fun, and it's not something that all of us are good at. This is why I suggested talking with a specialist and figuring out together the exact steps you should take.

But you know what's fun? The next chapter, in which we will talk about absolutely everything candle-crafting-related. That's right. Starting from this moment, we are going to dive into the juicy part of the business.

Chapter Four

Equipment, Supplies & Tools

L et's recap. You know the history, and you've scratched the surface of the science behind candles' burn. Furthermore, you are now very much up to date with all the necessary aspects for starting up the business.

Yet, I am pretty sure that you are well aware that knowing all the legal stuff and how to handle paperwork won't necessarily mean that you are ready to start producing your candles. No. To be more precise, bureaucracy is a means to an end, a necessary evil. However, the essential part of any candle crafting business is to have the correct equipment to work with.

So what do you think we should talk about next? If your answer is raw materials, then you are absolutely right. But let's recap a little. Remember how I told you that the burning process is different from one candle to another and that the wax type plays a significant role? Well, that's exactly right.

I learned the hard way that not working with the correct wax or wicks turns against you. To help you understand how important knowing how each resin type works, I will tell you a story.

So, do you recall how I told you that I ordered my first 'make your own candle kit?' I had no idea what I ordered. I just followed the instructions and ended up with a nice-smelling container candle. Therefore, I imagined that everything was just as easy. What do you think I did next?

I melted the candle and decided to create a votive. As you probably can imagine, the result was a disaster. The wax was too soft and, well, long story short, the candle was ugly, melted too fast, and smelled too powerfully.

It took me a long time to realize that the mistake was not melting the first candle but creating a product with the wrong wax. This is why it is vital to know each type of wax available on the market and the appropriate models to craft from them. Therefore, let's take a look at all wax types and understand their ups and downs as well as applications.

Candle Wax Types For You To Choose

As you've previously read, candle makers have been crafting candles using different resins throughout history. I know that I have mentioned them very briefly, so now I want to take the time and discuss each one. Thus, let's dive into the topic to understand more. I will start with one of the most popular types of wax, then will take you through the natural models only to end with a new type of material. But let's not linger any longer and get right to the point.

Paraffin wax

I will begin with this specific example because it is one of the most famous types of candle wax. The main reason for its popularity is its versatility. Because, yes, working with paraffin allows you to carry out many projects.

A fascinating fact about paraffin, one that not many people know, is that this compound has more than one melting point. Furthermore, paraffin can incorporate a significant amount of color or fragrance. And that is what makes it perfectly suitable for all types of projects. From containers to votives, paraffin can be your friend.

Naturally, due to its versatility and low cost, most commercial candles are manufactured using it.

When ordering your first paraffin kit, the only aspect you should consider is that this wax comes in two forms. The melting temperature point gives the difference between the two.

First of all, there is the 'low-melt-point paraffin' which melts at around 130 degrees Fahrenheit. It is a soft type of wax that works amazingly well when producing containers. Yet, I find that it is just as perfect for tealight candle manufacturing.

The second kind of paraffin is the 'high-melt-point paraffin.' As you probably imagine, this paraffin wax has a melting point greater than 130 degrees Fahrenheit. And since it has a higher melting point, it is more rigid and therefore perfect for crafting pillar candles or votives.

Anyway, as you probably heard, the oil industry is not the best for the environment. So, unfortunately, this wax has a couple of downsides, and the most important one is its lack of eco-friendliness. Because yes, since paraffin is a byproduct of the oil industry, the resin is not considered green, making many home crafters avoid it.

However, I will go ahead and suppose that you are at the beginning of the road. I will assume that you wish to learn more about making candles using a cheap material without thinking about other aspects while you perfect your technique. In that case, there is another thing you should know about paraffin.

If you don't take good care of your paraffin candle, choose a good quality wick, and trim it properly, you will end up with incomplete combustion. In other words, there will be too much fuel for your flame, and it will result in soot.

Luckily, there are other materials to choose from that are just as versatile as paraffin but have a less negative impact on the environment. Are you ready to check them out?

Soy wax

The next resin I want to talk about is made from soy. As you already know, soy wax has been discovered only in the last 30 years or so. Now, even though it is considered a new face in the scene, its popularity grows more by the day.

And that is one of the reasons I brought it up right after paraffin. Furthermore, like the up-mentioned resin, the soy one also has more than one melting point. Thus, it is considered to be just as flexible.

But the most remarkable thing about soy wax is that it is 100% natural, and therefore, it's a green choice.

I had many discussions with people asking me why one would pick soy wax when beeswax is such a great material to work with. I don't want to go into much detail regarding beeswax as we will very soon talk about it, but I want to say only one thing. Yes, beeswax is terrific, but it's also costly, and of course, as many of you will say, it's not vegan. Therefore soy wax is a great natural wax, cheaper than other types, and 100% vegan. Furthermore, the material is easy to work with, making it very simple to produce candles that burn slowly and clean. So, these are the main reasons why I would recommend it.

But, as always there are also some negative aspects that you should know. For instance, there are more and more concerns about the fertilizers and pesticides used to grow soybeans. Therefore, it may be a natural substance, but it also can provoke damage to the environment if the plantations don't respect the correct norms.

Another backside of using soy wax would be its capacity to hold fragrance. Yet, this can be a plus for people who wish to have just a slight hint of odor.

All clear so far? Great. Now, let's move on to the actual soy wax production.

So, as its name implies, this resin is made out of soybeans' oil. The plant is grown to maturity and then harvested. After that, it's a straightforward method of cleaning the beans, craking, de-hulling and rolling them into flakes. Only then does the oil gets extracted. Yet, it cannot be used as it is. Thus, it goes through a process of hydrogenation, converting fatty acids into saturated ones. Thanks to these chemical treatments, the melting point is altered, transforming the oil into a solid.

Now, it is for you to decide if soy wax is worth using or not. Many manufacturers love it, and just as many claims that its hype is not justified.

Anyhow, my personal advice is to try it and see how working with it feels.

Palm wax

If you Google candle waxes, you will most likely stumble upon palm wax. Even though I don't support it and never work with this wax, I feel obliged to talk about it and understand why I think the way I do.

So, palm wax is somehow very similar to soy resin. It's 100% natural and vegan. Moreover, it's a firm wax that works amazingly for crafting pillars or votives.

Another great benefit would be its almost crystalline visual effect which gives candles an amazing appearance. Furthermore, it holds color and fragrances very well. Plus, it produces almost no soot since it burns perfectly clean.

Therefore one might be inclined to say that this wax is indeed the perfect one for producing candles. I mean, it is more expensive than others, but it's worth it, right? Well, no.

Unfortunately, palm wax has a huge disadvantage - it's not environmentally friendly. And before you jump from your seat and say that I'm clearly crazy since I recently mentioned that palm wax is 100% vegan and natural, I want you to let me explain all implications.

When palm wax was discovered, it was considered a truly magical material. And for good reasons, I might add.

Long story short, this wax is obtained by harvesting palm tree oil. Since I am sure that I don't need to draw you a picture of how this tree looks, I will skip describing its appearance. However, I will tell you that the oil is extracted from the tree's red fruits. If you are curious about the actual extraction procedure, I can tell you in a few words how it is done.

First of all, the fruit's flesh is destroyed and pressed. Doing so, the manufacturers release the oil, which has a very pleasant reddish look. Next, just as in soy wax's case, the compound goes under a hydrogenation process that turns it from liquid to solid.

Suppose the final product is designed for candle making. In that case, manufacturers bleach it, turning the radish color into white.

So far, so good, right?

Well, yes, as I've said, palm wax is the best material to work with at first glance. Unfortunately, many environmental problems simply can't be overlooked.

Let me go back in time, so I can better explain the situation in words that you can understand my point of view.

Scientists discovered palm oil somewhere around the 20th century. Until then, palm trees were simply ornamental plants - coconut trees without the coconuts. Anyway, after realizing the potential behind palm oil, countries such as Indonesia and Malaysia, but also throughout the whole African continent, started to grow these trees on a huge scale. This means that they needed more and more land to farm. In order to do that, they slashed and burned entire forests, making way for palm trees. In other words, farming palm trees created reasons for massive deforestation.

Naturally, many people tried to find solutions. I mean, it's in no one's interest to destroy the habitat of numerous animals and plants.

Therefore, giant companies struggled to keep palm farms within some limits and not to endanger even more species.

However, there is one very big problem. Cultivating the same land over and over again reduces the soil's fertility level. Simply put, in a couple of years, that piece of land becomes useless for a very long time.

In recent years, an organization called the Roundtable for Sustainable Palm Oil started to make genuine efforts to find better solutions for growing palm trees.

But until something changes in this direction, I cannot promote the use of palm wax for crafting candles.

This being said, with all the natural resins out of the way, we are down to just one, the king and queen of all waxes - the beeswax.

Beeswax

Beeswax has been around since the beginning of time. It is the most natural form of resin, and that is why many consider it the most suitable for crafting candles.

However, just as in all cases, I want to get into more details to help you really understand what makes each wax unique.

So, maybe you know this already, but I will tell you nevertheless. Beeswax is the byproduct that bees make when producing their honey. In other words, you simply can't harvest honey without taking the wax as well.

But how do bees produce beeswax? Well, it's very interesting and simple at the same time. The little flying creatures excrete this substance and use it to incubate their larvae. Now, what I find extremely fascinating about this process is that not all beeswax smell the same. Yes, you read that right.

We all know that beeswax leaves a sweet natural odor. This is possible because it's infused with honey. However, not many are aware that the beeswax' smell differs from one beehive to the next. The reason? It depends on what type of plants or flowers those bees feed on.

So the beekeeper takes the honey and the wax out. Then what? After harvesting the natural product from the beehive, the wax is melted then filtered. This process repeats a couple of times until you are left with a nice and clean compound. Finally, the product is placed in blocks or slabs, pre-rolled sheets, or pastillas.

Great! Now let's focus a bit on the pros and cons of using beeswax. You know by now that I try to be as positive as possible. Therefore, I will start with the so many pluses beeswax has.

First of all, I will highlight the most obvious reason - it's 100% natural and doesn't need too much processing after harvesting.

With this not-questionable part out of the way, let me tell you a funny story that will highlight another benefit lighting beeswax candles give.

When I first started to make candles and tried my first beeswax model, I immediately remembered something from my childhood.

I remembered how, when I was a kid, my grandmother used to light beeswax candles each evening. It was not for light, and it was definitely not for any atmospheric purposes because she was not at all into that kind of stuff.

I personally loved the smell and couldn't take my eyes off the beautiful flame. Yet, she didn't care too much for it. Finally, I asked her why did she light candles if she didn't like them. Her answer was not very straightforward, but I let it go since I was very young. I can still see the image of her doing her daily chores in the kitchen when she turned to me and said, 'for the mold.' As I said, I didn't understand, and since it didn't matter to me very much, I moved my focus back to my toys.

However, many years later, more than I like to admit, when I started to read and learn about each wax, I realized that there was actually truth behind granny's words. Yes, it is scientifically proven that lighting beeswax candles in a room can prevent forming of yeasts and fungi. So yeah, my grandmother was right all along, and I had no idea about it. I just thought it was one of her crazy superstition things.

Anyhow, their antifungal properties are not the only reason why people love beeswax candles.

As I said earlier, these candles smell delicious without adding any other fragrance. Furthermore, they tend to have different aromas based on the place where the wax was harvested from. Another aspect worth mentioning is the wax's natural preserver features. But what does that mean? It means that beeswax never goes bad. And the substance which ensures this 'forever lasting' aspect is none other than propolis.

I am sure that if you ever suffered from a sore throat, the doctor's chances of prescribing you lozenges with propolis are extremely high. Even so, I will explain in a couple of sentences what propolis is and why it is so amazing.

First of all, the word "propolis" comes from a Greek word that means 'defense of the city." The reason for the name choice is very straightforward - the main job propolis has is to strengthen the beehive, working as an antiseptic barrier. Now, imagine how powerful propolis is if unspoiled beeswax was found in ancient tombs.

This being said, beeswax is truly amazing from every point of view.

However, this super-wax has some downsides as well. Probably, the biggest minus people think when talking about beeswax is its animal provenance. In other words, it is not vegan. Therefore, it raises some discussions regarding cruelty-free aspects. I don't want to go into many details on the matter, but I will add that, unfortunately, harvesting beeswax at a large scale is not always done by the book.

Of course, some ethical suppliers put bees' safety first, not harming them in the harvesting process. But, naturally, they sell their merchandise at higher prices.

This being said, let's take small yet steady steps and move from natural waxes and back to a chemical compound.

Candle gel wax

The last type of wax you can consider using for candle crafting is gel wax. Well, technically speaking, this is not a wax per se but a mix of mineral oil and resin.

When it comes to its characteristics, gel wax has really great capacities for retaining color and fragrances. Basically, the same as other waxes. However, this one here is transparent, allowing you to let your creativity go wild and create crazy candles.

How are you? Did you manage to accumulate enough information, and most importantly, did you understand the difference between waxes?

If you still have parts that don't seem crystal clear, don't worry. It's normal. Knowing the theory perfectly won't make you a great practitioner, regardless of your profession. You have to really put your shoulder to work and get your hands dirty to understand the secrets behind each resin. And neither I nor anybody else can teach you the technique if you don't practice. But I can tell you that knowing how to master waxes is not the only secret in this business. You won't manage to craft the perfect candle if you don't use the appropriate wick.

And that is exactly our next point of discussion.

Candle Wicks

So, candle wicks? They seem so unimportant, right? I mean, it's that piece of fabric that you simply light to heat up the wax. Or is it more than meets the eye? Yes, wicks are extremely important and can ruin your candle if you don't take them seriously.

When I explained to you the science behind candles, I told you that the wick is the one delivering fuel for the flame. Remember? It doesn't matter if you don't because I will repeat this part just to be sure you don't finish this book without having all the vital information you were looking for when deciding to read it.

So the reason why candles have wicks is that they need a 'fuel pump.' The sole purpose of wicks is to transport the liquid wax into the flame, feeding it.

Naturally, depending on the size and material of the wick, they can produce different results. Needless to say that you want to discover the perfect wick for each candle. If not, you might find yourself producing too much fuel and therefore soot or too little fuel and a sputtering flame.

The good news is that today you can find any kind of wick you could wish for. The bad news is that there are hundreds of different models to choose from, and every characteristic of the wax influences the way the wick delivers.

Simply put, selecting the right wick is a critical step, so you should not treat it superficially. Therefore, let's see what you will be facing when deciding on the matter of ordering your 'fuel pumps.'

One of the most important aspects you will need to take into account when choosing your wick is its burn rate.

In simple words, this term refers to how many grams of wax are consumed by the wick in an hour. As you can easily deduct, the higher the rate, the more burned wax. Each manufacturer provides a burn rate, but from my experience, you should not trust it blindly. Do burn tests for each batch you buy. This way, you make sure that the results are the exact ones you seek.

Another crucial feature that you need to really look into is the wax consumption rate. Depending on the wick you will choose, this rate is different. For instance, a loose braid consumes more fuel than a tighter braid, and that is a fact even if they are manufactured using the same raw materials. Again, this part can only be discovered by practicing and working with every component you can put your hand on.

Doing so, you will most probably end up having at least one case of a smoking wick. Because yes, if you choose your wick correctly, it should not be smokey. So then, why do you think this happens?

Well, in most cases, this is a sign of using a wick that is too large for your candle. Trying to light a candle with such an inappropriate wick will consume more melted wax than what the flame can burn efficiently. As a result, you will be left with unburned materials that will either smoke or soot.

The final problem an unsuitable wick can cause is something known as mushrooming. Now, regardless of what others will tell you, there is more than one reason why this can occur.

Of course, cored wicks, which we will talk about shortly, are more likely to present this problem. The explanation behind this is simple. Cored wicks are rigid and tend to burn in cooler parts of the flame.

However, you can notice this issue with other wicks, so again, the best thing you can do is to test test test. Yes, test everything twice even more before you declare yourself convinced.

Okay? Great! Now let's see what are the most frequently used wicks so you can at least make an idea of what to buy for the type of candles you wish to craft.

Cotton Wicks

First of all, you need to understand that traditional wicks can be divided into two big categories - cotton and wooden wicks.

Of course, there are subcategories that I will tell you about shortly. But until then, let's discuss the general characteristics of cotton wicks so you can understand exactly what makes them special.

So, cotton wicks are made out of braided fibers that ensure the flame ignites properly. These wicks can even be crafted at home, dipping the braided fibers into a solution containing borax, salt, and water. Yet, I don't really advise you to go as far. Especially not at the beginning of your career. Because if you end up with fragile wicks, you won't get good results.

Anyhow, let's return to the commercial ones. As you will soon read, there are many subcategories of cotton-made wicks, and each of them can be purchased even in more than one color.

As you can probably guess, just as when choosing your wax, there are advantages and disadvantages that you have to be aware of.

One of the many pluses cotton wicks provide is their great capacity for fast lighting. Yes, these wicks tend to light in less than 4 seconds. Furthermore, you can light them with whatever you want, including matches.

Cotton wicks are also the best choice for outdoor candles. They won't stand still in front of a great wind, but they can handle some gusts better than other alternatives, at least.

Now, for me, the main reason why I like to work with cotton wicks is that they are super versatile. You can find an appropriate model for any kind of project you have in mind. Furthermore, not only are they very suited for scented candles, but you might even find some cotton wicks that have their own fragrance.

However, there are also some downsides when it comes to these wicks. First and foremost, they are not very sustainable. To ensure good self-trimming, manufacturers may use materials such as lead or zinc. Moreover, some cotton wicks are crafted using paraffin wax. All these chemicals are used to ensure their safety and an even burn, but they make these wicks less eco-friendly than one might think.

Anyhow, you will more likely than not use cotton wicks, so let's take a look at all the models you can buy and discuss which one is suitable for what project.

Flat Wicks

Flat wicks are very popular among candle crafters. They are designed to bend a little when they burn. Due to this fact, they are not very prone to create the mushrooming effect I was telling you about. Simply put, their curling gives a self-trimming outcome.

Now, if you are curious about the material used to manufacture these wicks, most often than not, they come made from three bundles of fiber.

Finally, the best application for these wicks is a free-standing candle. So if you are into crafting pillars or tapers, these wicks will work just fine.

Square Wicks

The next very popular wick type is the squared one. Like the previous model, square wicks are also a great choice for pillars or tapers. The reason is mostly the same - the wick bends a little when burning.

Truth be told, the robustness level makes a big difference between them. Square wicks are more robust than flat ones, making them perfect for when working with beeswax.

Cored Wicks

Even though I told you that these wicks could cause issues such as mushrooming, they still remain a great choice for many projects such as votives or jar candles.

These wicks come either knitted or braided, and they use a core material that is meant to keep them straight while burning. This core can be made from more than one material, but it comes from cotton, zinc, or paper.

However, to ensure a good burn, it is recommended to pre-wax these wicks. This process increases the rigidity, making them more supportive.

HTP Wick

The three types of wicks that I started with are the most frequently used ones, but there are other types you should know about. For instance, this model is a mix between flat wicks and cored ones, combining their self-trimming and rigidity properties.

In other words, they are not very prone to mushrooming and can be used for any kind of wax you can think of, including gel.

Performa Coreless Wicks

The Performa Coreless Wicks are not very easy to work with, in my opinion, but they are great for difficult applications. They are made very similar to flat wicks but are also created in such a way to resist bending when burning.

I can only advise you to leave these wicks for when you have enough experience and use them for viscous waxes that need a more robust flame.

LX Wicks

This is another example of special wicks that are great and beloved by advanced users. LX wicks are a mix between flat wicks and coreless ones. Their main characteristic is slightly bending when burning without any mushrooming effect.

They help crafters to produce candles with consistent flame and no soot. As for applications, you can probably use these wicks for any waxes, but I suggest trying them for pillars or containers.

RRD Wicks

The manufacturers that made LX wicks possible also gave us the marvelous RRD wicks. Basically, these ones here are cored and are capable of burning viscous materials without clogging. Therefore, these wicks are a great choice for votives or containers with a high volume of fragrance.

I personally love these wicks because of their capacity to burn with a slight curl yet with a constant and consistent flame.

CD Wicks

Finally, the CD type is the last cotton wick model that I want to tell you about. These are coreless, flat wicks that have a special paper filament.

The beauty of these wicks stands in their versatility as they have the power to melt any kind of wax and keep a consistent burn regardless of the resin.

Wooden Wicks

Up until now, we talked only about cotton-made wicks. However, there are also ones made of wood. These wicks are quite new and are gaining popularity by the day. They are so beloved due to their visual appeal as well as the sound they create when they burn. When you light up a candle that has a wooden wick, it is almost as if something is crackling in the back.

Furthermore, wooden wicks are a more natural and eco-friendly alternative to cotton ones. To give you a more visual description of these wicks, think about slim woody slabs. Now, before you go and assume that you could use any kind of slim wood, the answer is no. These are specially designed for this purpose.

When it comes to their applications, manufacturers will tell you that they are suitable for any kind of wax. Yet, my personal opinion is that they go best with paraffin, soy, and gel wax. My advice to you is to try them out and see how you like working with them based on the wax you choose.

Anyhow, moving on, I can tell you that there are two types of wooden wicks you can choose from. There are single or dual wicks. The difference between the two is given by the number of wooden pieces the wick has.

What I mostly like about these wicks is their crazy fragrance. You don't have to use oils or other odors for your candles. The wicks alone will give you that cozy smell of a fireplace. Therefore, I mostly use wooden wicks for calming candles. I find that lighting a wooden wick candle really takes the stress away. Again, this is just my opinion, and you should not take my word for it.

Without any reason or doubt, you should believe that wood wicks are 100% eco-friendly. Yes, even though they are made of wood, they are made only from sustainable wood. This means that no forest or environment is being harmed for their manufacturing.

Besides, compared to cotton wicks, these ones here don't need any harmful chemicals for their well-being. They produce an even burn by themselves, leaving no residual wax behind.

Now, if you are like me and like to look at the candle's flame and get lost in your thoughts, then you should know that wood wicks will help you create a beautiful horizontal flame that burns slowly and steadily.

Of course, using wooden wicks is not always peach.

They need some maintenance and special attention. For instance, wooden wicks' candles can't be lit with a match. You need a lighter to do so. The reason? The match doesn't burn for enough time to allow the wood to ignite. You will end up with a burned match before the flame can settle in. Not only is this frustrating, but it can also produce damage due to the debris left on the wax.

Furthermore, if you don't wait for the flame to stabilize its burn, you will end up with a candle that doesn't melt the wax properly. This can mean that your candle will only burn in the middle, creating something known as 'a tunnel.' And I don't need to tell you that customers hate when this happens.

Anyway, I am not saying that all these can't be figured out and create beautiful candles with wooden wicks. Some crafters even claim that using wooden wicks is easier thanks to their stable position. That is true. However, these wicks burn a little bit differently than cotton ones, so you better make sure that you know exactly what you are doing before adventuring into such a project.

Hemp Wicks

This next category is one that is under some kind of controversy. And I will tell you exactly why.

Long story short, many crafters don't even consider working with these wicks as they are mostly used for bongs and pipes. Simply put, people use them to smoke weed, actually, for lighting up their joints or whatever.

Anyway, there is more to this type of wick than what forums mostly tell you about it.

So a hemp wick is a twine made using only natural hemp fibers that are then covered in beeswax. Basically, these wicks work as standalone candlesticks.

If you bypass the whole smoking weed aspect, you might actually find that using these wicks brings loads of advantages. For instance, they are 100% organic. This means that they don't contain any chemicals or plastic, or pesticides. Another very big advantage is the beeswax coat I was telling you about. So, they are basically ready to use out of the pocket.

As for their burning capacities, hemp wicks burn with a large flame, malting the wax smoothly and even as it burns.

Finally, these wicks have the right rigidity, allowing you to work easily while anchoring them.

Now, as far as applications go, I would recommend using hemp wicks for smaller candles such as tea ones. But then again, it's just a matter of preference.

I am almost positive that your head is spinning by now with all the information. I promise that I will return to the topic and tell you how to combine waxes and wicks best. Yet I want you to really chew on everything that you just read. Doing so will allow you to really understand what I will be talking about in the next chapter.

But until then, let's look at another very important aspect of creating the perfect candle, which is fragrance.

Candle Fragrances

Loved by many people but also problematic when it comes to others, scented candles are a big hit nonetheless.

We refer to scented candles as the ones that use some kind of fragrance oils in their composition and not the naturally scented ones, such as beeswax candles.

People who like smelling candles will tell you that they use one in any room of their home. I have a friend that has a different scent in each room as she says that each one suits the decorations and the style. Just to give you an idea, she has a lavender-scented candle in her bedroom that has the role of calming her before going to bed, she has a lilly one in the bathroom to create an almost spa feeling and a vanilla one in the kitchen because, as she says 'If I can't bake at least this way my kitchen smells like pie.'

So yes, scented candles have the power of creating the right atmosphere if you know how to use them properly. On the other hand, they can be a total disaster if they are too strong fragranced or the person buying them doesn't like that specific smell. For instance, I hate the smell of caramel. Yes, that's right. For me, caramel candles are a total no-no. And that's okay. We are unique characters, and luckily for us, we live in an era in which these small preferences actually matter and can be met easily.

But let's return to the scented candles. When I first started to even consider founding my business, my mother asked me why people would buy my fragranced candles when they could use incense for the smell. I have to admit that at first, she blocked me. I had to think really hard about a reason. I even went to buy some incense to figure out why I like candles more. Of course, I am crazy and like to look at the flame, but usually, people are not like me. However, I very soon got my answer. Incense is smokey, while a well-made scented candle will not leave any smoke trace in the air.

I was so happy that I got my answer that I called my mom in the middle of the night to let her know why she should buy my product. Of course, she was not very happy for waking her up and scaring the soul out of her, but she got over it the next morning and agreed with me.

But let's go past my crazy family and me and focus on what truly matters: actually crafting scented candles.

Now, truth be told, there is more than one way to do so. And I will tell you right from the start that the first try might be a disaster. I personally needed some time until I reached the perfect scented candles. My main issue was the actual smell. When I smelled the wax without the candle being lit, I was very happy with the result, but there was not a single scent in the air once I lighted the candle. You know me by now enough to understand that I was going crazy with frustration.

I only later found out that I was using some poorly pre-blended wax with its own saturation point for the fragrance oil. So even though I kept adding more oil, it was more than what my wax was able to absorb. The extra was just sweated out and wasted.

If you want to know the science behind this absorption rate, even though you will discover it yourself, you should know that a pre-blended wax can absorb between 15-30 ml of oil per 0.45 kg wax.

Anyway, don't fuss about remembering these numbers. It all depends on the type of wax you use.

What I want you to remember at this point is that you can create any variety of scented candles you want.

Another thing that you should understand right now is that well-done scented candles have the capacity to release their aroma even when they are unlit. However, that is a very discrete smell that can only be felt when you hold such a candle in your hand.

Now, the real odor is delivered when burning, and it's done thanks to evaporation. Basically, nothing new happens when you light a scented candle. As you already know, you light the wick, and it gives heat. After that, the heat melts the wax and all that jazz. Now, because the aroma is an integrated part of wax, the odor is released when it melts. And that is why the longer the candle burns, the more fragrance is being released.

Great! But how does the aroma get to become part of the wax, you might wonder? Well, this is no rocket science. You just mix the liquid wax with your preferred scented mixture.

And now the answer to the question I am sure you have in mind - what are my choices when it comes to the scented mixture.

I want you to understand that big brands and home crafters alike work for years to create unique fragrances to attract their clients. In other words, regardless of what you will use for scenting your candles, you will need to find a way to make it stand out, to be your signature mark. You will have to play with aromas until you can't stand smelling another perfume. And unfortunately, nobody will teach you how to create this part. As I said, fragrances are the best-kept secret of each candle crafter. So, if you are here to discover how to develop the perfect smell, I will have to disappoint you. You won't be able to read about this part in this book. However, you will learn about the ingredients you can choose from, and I will share my opinion on each of them.

Anyhow, until I start explaining all your options when it comes to scenting your wax, I want to give you some advice.

As you will see, there is more than one way to make your candles smell nice. Some of them are natural picks, while others are not so much. I will tell you about everything, but I can only highlight to try and stick as much as possible close to natural fragrances. You don't want to create synthetic aromas and sell your products to people who are allergic to that chemical compound. It can backfire in so many ways.

Anyway, you will have to choose to use either essential oils or fragranced ones at the end of the day. Now, the latter can be either natural or synthetic sources. This being said, as always, I will take each possibility and tell you everything there is to know about it, with its good and bad parts.

Essential oils

Essential oils are very highly concentrated liquids extracted from various plants. As you can imagine, these oils contain a very strong scent, more potent than one of the plants itself.

Well, due to their natural provenience, using essential oils won't make your candle keep a very profound smell. Rather than a concentrated fragrance, essential oils help candles burn with a more delicate odor.

Another thing that you should be aware of before you start crafting candles using essential oils is that you may not end up with the same level of fragrance each time. Depending on the plants used for the oil extraction, the final product can be more concentrated or diluted. And since no chemicals are involved, it's just the way it is. You might discover that you'll have to use a larger amount of oil to achieve the desired scent intensity. But using essential oils has more than the natural advantage. For instance, essential oils have a very good shelf life. Therefore, the candles crafted with essential oils also have a good shelf life. Now, I can't give you a precise period as they differ from one essential oil to the next. However, you should expect them to last somewhere between 2 and 5 years. Furthermore, some oils are derived from specific types of organic matter. These ones can last up to 15 years, if not more.

Now, my personal advice for you regarding the matter is to use essential oils when crafting container candles with a lid. Sealing the scent when the candle is not lit will keep the fragrance rich for a longer period of time. The explication behind this suggestion is simple to understand. Essential oils tend to break down when they are in contact with direct light and oxygen. So by simply adding a lid, you stop evaporation.

All clear so far? Great! Now, let's move to the other type of oils you can find on the market.

Fragrance oils

Fragrance oils are very concentrated oils that contain either natural or synthetic aromas.

There are many differences between the two oil types, yet the main one is that you don't need the actual plant to extract fragrance oils. Furthermore, they are more powerful and more stable than essential ones. Therefore, fragrance oils or more reliable when used for sentencing your wax.

Let me explain exactly what I mean.

Each drop of fragrance oil will always have the same smell concentration. And as you already know, the situation is different with essential oils. What is even more important is that if you take a drop of Chamomile essential oil and a drop of Chamomile fragrance oil, the letter will be more potent.

Now, there is a false misconception when it comes to fragrance oils. Many people say that since they are synthetic made, they are not safe to use. Well, let me tell you that this here is a big fat lie. In other words, that's false.

Fragrance oils are perfectly safe when it comes to aromatizing your candles.

As a matter of fact, many essential oils can provoke skin allergies if you don't handle them correctly.

Anyway, to wrap the matter up and move to the next part of the discussion, I can honestly say that both oil types are more than safe to be used when crofting candles. Furthermore, both versions smell great if you use them properly.

The only difference I can think of is regarding the supply costs and therefore the price you can charge for your candles. But that's a conversation for a different day. Now, we have more pressing topics to talk about. So let's move on!

Color

I don't know how other people are, but for me, it's very important to have a good connection between smell and color. And that is not only when it comes to candles.

I mean, think about eating a strawberry pie. You don't want it to be blue, green, or yellow. No. You want your pie to be red. Am I right?

So just as I love my pies to be the right color, and God knows I do love pies, I also like my candles to follow the same rule. And since you can't color the wax without some kind of dye, this is exactly what we will be talking about next.

Before you choose any candle dye, you will have to take into consideration more than one factor. My suggestion is to look at them one by one and understand them.

Pigments or Dyes

I want to highlight right from the start that there is two major dyestuffs to choose from and that two choices are pigments or dyes. The thing about them is that you should make a clear distinction between the two or you can find yourself in a lot of trouble.

The first category, pigments, represents an insoluble inorganic substance that won't dissolve in a mixture. In contrast, pigments sit in as a suspension. This means that if not done right, you will end up with the particles clogging on the wick, making it impossible to reach a perfect burning and, therefore, increasing the risk of combustion.

Basically, I don't recommend pigments for your candle crafting. This also includes things such as mica powder, titanium dioxide, or crayons. Many of them are marketed as candle dye, but I strongly believe that you should only use them to color your candle's exterior.

On the other hand, dyes are compounds soluble in oil. This means that they are perfect for giving color to your candles.

But what are dyes? They are mostly made out of synthetic compounds by the name of aniline. When mixed with the wax, dyes create an emulsion that allows an even color and smooth burn. Therefore, dyes are the most natural choice.

But as you can imagine, there's more to the topic than meets the eye.

Dye Types

I will talk to you about the amount of color you should use in a jiffy, but until then, you should know how many dye types are available on the market.

Because I did learn the hard way that you should not take each type of dye for granted and use it blindly, without further ado, let's take each model at a time and see their characteristics.

Dye Blocks and Chips

Basically, these dyes have just one major difference between them, and that is their size. So as you can probably imagine, the chips are the smaller version, while the blocks are, well, naturally bigger. Either way, they represent pre-colored wax or a wax-soluble material.

As you can imagine, chips are perfect for when you craft small batches of candles, while blocks are, of course, for bigger batches.

So the way they work is simple. You measure the amount you need, and you place it in the melted wax. They will melt and combine, coloring the wax. Of course, you can even mix colors to create your own color or shade. Now, a word of advice. These dyes go amazing for paraffin waxes. Therefore, it is a good idea to start with this resin.

Anyway, even though this coloring option is beloved by almost all crafters, there is a little bit of downside you should know about. If you are not careful and don't stir enough to mix them right, you will have a settlement at the bottom of your candle. But other than that, you should really like working with these dyes.

Liquid Dyes

This is another form of synthetic dye. But compared to the other type of dye we just talked about, liquid dyes are not suitable for all kinds of wax. The reason for that is because they are really concentrated. I personally use it only for soy wax, but you can test and see if you like to mix it with other resins.

These liquid dyes are usually sold in bottles with dropper lids, making them perfect for mixing colors. Now my advice to you is to write down the number of drops you use whenever you try to create a new color. This way, you will know exactly how to recreate or adapt it.

<u>Powdered Dyes</u>

Now, speaking of concentrated dyes, you have one last alternative: powdered dyes. These dyes are amazing, and if used right, they create beautiful colors with just the smallest quantity.

However, they can also be very messy, and if you are not careful, you will color yourself and everything around you. Plus, you need to use a little bit of powder at a time. If not, you may notice clumps all over your wax, and you don't want that.

Yes, using a powder dye is not very easy, and you should not start experimenting with it right at the beginning of the road. Wait to gain some experience before you begin using it, but don't neglect it because these dyes produce fabulous chromatics.

Anyway, just as with the liquid version, write down the amount you use in order to get consistent colors each time.

No matter how good the dye you use, you will need to learn how to use it. This is why we shall move the topic to something known as color saturation. Don't worry if you don't know what I mean because I will explain everything.

Color saturation

In very simple words, color saturation is the fancy way of saying color intensity. So, basically, you need to know how much dye to use in order to create beautiful candles. And the most problematic part is to understand the color saturation level for each type of dye. Because yes, different types of dyes will produce different levels of color.

As you have already read, there are more or less concentrated possibilities. And in order to be constant with your products, you will need to establish a color saturation and repeat the process every time. Remember how I told you to write down the quantities? That is exactly what you have to do.

Furthermore, you should not try to recreate a color with different types of dyes. Trust me! It won't work. And the reason for that is very easy to understand. Different types of dyes have different concentrations. What am I saying? Even if you buy red, for example, from different brands, you will still get distinctive results.

Just as with fragrances, each crafter has their little secrets that they won't share. And it's totally normal. These are the little things that make you and your business unique.

Nevertheless, I want to whisper some of my private techniques that will help you start creating some shading of your own.

So as you can imagine, I had some terrible results trying to create unique colors. And I don't mean only at the beginning of my road. No. I had very bad outcomes even in recent years. Therefore, here are the basic aspects that you should try and follow.

When you try to create a color, never start with a big amount of color from the start. That might turn out to be a disaster. Instead, start with a very small amount and go from there. To make sure that you are on the right track, my advice is to coat the back of a spoon in wax then dip it into ice water. When the wax gets cold and hard, it will show its true color.

If you think that you got a winner, then test it on a different type of wax. You might be amazed to see how different things can look.

Anyway, before going into the 'independent' approach, you should follow the manufacturer's directions as they will guide you through the process.

This being said, I want to move our focus to another topic. There are a few precautions you will need to take when working with dyes because, of course, accidents can happen.

Firstly, you should be careful what dye you buy. There are many very poor-quality brands, which can end up being quite dangerous. I found more than one occasion in which the dye was actually an insoluble pigment. And since the last thing you want is to increase the risk of combustion, you should avoid them

The second precaution I can think of right now is to always work without gloves because it will be a pain in your butt to get the dye stains off your skin. But that's not all. There are people that have allergies that they have no idea about. I can only assume that it's not nice to end up at the hospital full of dye and with a bad rash.

Yet, your hands are not the only things that need protection. Your workspace is just as important. If you are not careful, you will have a countertop full of stains. For this purpose, you can use whatever protection you want. However, I love to use newspapers or old sheets.

Finally, I hope that I don't need to highlight this, but I will mention it nevertheless. Never, under any circumstances, leave the dyes open within reach of pets or children. They are 100% toxic if eaten.

And since we reach this discussion point, it is only natural to address a question that many of you probably wonder - are candle dyes safe?

Yes, they are safe. If used right, they should not raise any medical concern. When I say to use right, you should understand that there's no rocket science around my words. You just have to follow the manufacturer's instructions and keep the dye away from your mouth. In other words, I am talking about basic survival skills.

As we move forward from the color topic, there is just one matter to discuss and that is storing the dyes.

Storage

The most important thing you need to know regarding this aspect is that no matter what dye you'll buy, they are all sensitive to UV light. Yet, moisture doesn't help them either.

Of course, there are some special additives that are called UV inhibitors. You can use them while you work with the dye, especially if you have your working studio in direct sunlight. Using such a product will ensure that the color doesn't fade and keeps its fresh aspect.

Anyhow, the best advice I can give you is to store your dyes in a cool, dry, and dark place.

In essence, this sums up everything you need to know about color. The rest is up for you to experiment and explore. I can guarantee you that it's impossible not to find your way and discover unique chromatics and turn them into your signature.

And speaking of uniqueness, let's see what other equipment you need to create beautiful, one-of-the-kind candles.

Containers

Candle containers are just as essential as wax and wicks. Over the years, I talked with people who took this road and became candle-maker entrepreneurs. Most of them claim that they still prefer using jam jars. And I can't blame them as these containers are indeed amazing, especially when you are at the beginning of the road.

Truth be told, you can use any kind of container you like as long as it's fireproof, won't crack, and doesn't leak.

Now, as straightforward as this might sound, I was actually shocked hearing some unfortunate stories. This is why I want to elaborate on the topic a little bit more.

Fireproof and cracking containers - I know that many of you will think I'm crazy to talk about this, but in fact, this is a very important topic. Therefore, I won't skip it. The most frequent mistake many people make is to think that any glass recipient is suited to be used as a candle container. Well, I won't linger too much on the matter and tell you that is not.

Most likely than not, using inappropriate vessels will simply make them crack. If this happens, you will find yourself in a situation you simply don't want - hot wax spills. And that my friends can be dangerous. Contrary to what you may think, getting a hot wax burn is not the only concern you should have. Actually, if the container cracks, a very big issue is caused by the wick. What could happen is that the wax-rooted wick can create an increased flame if it's left in a no-wax pool. And you don't want to start a fire.

But then again, there are other aspects to be taken into consideration. For instance, not only glass containers can cause problems but also ceramic ones. The issue with these vessels is that they are porous and can soak up the wax. The result? Again, a giant flame and a high risk of setting things on fire.

I hope that I don't need to highlight the fact that no plastic or other burning materials are out of the question.

About leaking aspects, you already know that it's a dangerous situation. So what you should know is that lousy metal tins are most likely to leak. Therefore, you should never use such a vessel without testing it. But you should definitely take them into consideration.

My advice to you is to fill the tin with water and let it sit for a couple of days. If it doesn't leak, then it's safe to use. So what kind of jars should you consider?

In my opinion, candle tins jars are very high-quality containers with a smooth texture. They usually have a round shape and come in many sizes and colors. What I like the best about tin cans is that I can reuse them. Basically, what I try to say is that you can use the tins as many times as you like, mainly if you offer discounts for returning old tins.

I actually know people that prefer them to glass jars because they resist more and have a forgiving nature.

In any words, candle tins are very adaptable and can be reused for multiple purposes after the candle has entirely burned. Even if your customers don't send you the tins back, you can teach them how to be eco-friendly and turn them into jewelry containers, shop presents, party favors, and even store herbs, balms, and gels.

So what else do you think it's important to be aware of? Well, you already know that a container has to be fire resistant and should not leak. But there are other aspects to consider. First and foremost, you need to use a container that is big enough for your candle. Having the flame too close to the edge of the container is just as dangerous as the other parts I told you about earlier.

Furthermore, the containers don't have to be narrowed at the bottom. If you use a vessel that has a wide mouth but a narrow bottom, you can produce too much heat that can crack the glass. Anyhow, before moving on, I need to say that regardless of what kind of containers you use, you should definitely test it.

Let me tell you what I do when I choose a new vessel. After I craft the candle, I light it up and let it burn for a couple of hours on a heat-resistant surface. If the container is still good, then I move to the actual production.

However, you should never forget the most important thing, which is safety first! Don't you ever light the candle and leave it unattended.

Molds

I am sure that by now you are asking yourself - what about crafting candles that don't require a container? Well, in this case, you will need to use some kind of mold. There is more than one type of mold, and I will tell you everything about each category.

Metal Candle Molds

These are the first types of molds that were ever created. Actually, they were made out of tin back then, but now they are mostly made out of aluminum.

The beauty of metal molds is that if you take good care of them, you will be able to use them for a very long time. The only thing about these molds is that you will need to use a mold release spray. It's very simple to apply. You just spray it inside the mold before pouring the hot wax. Remember that you should repeat this process before every wax pour.

The problem with these molds is that you might find it difficult to get out your finished product, especially if you don't have a strong grip.

Anyway, I can give you a tip I learned in time. If you have a problem removing the candle from the mold, I recommend placing the mold in the freezer for 15 minutes.

Plastic Candle Molds

If you want something that is not made of metal, then you could go with plastic models. Now the thing about plastic molds is that they are not suited for all wax types. So before anything else, you should make sure that your mold goes with your wax. The last thing you want is to melt your mold when you pour the hot wax into it.

Now the good thing about plastic molds is that they are not that expensive. But then again, they are not very sturdy.

Just as with metal molds, you will need to use a release spray to take the candle out easily. Furthermore, not using a spray might even make the mold crack, so you should not even consider working without one.

Silicone Candle Molds

The last category of mold that you can use is made out of silicone.

I can say for sure that silicone molds are very loved, especially in the beeswax community. The reason is very simple to understand. Their rubbery texture is super flexible and comes in all shapes and sizes. Furthermore, they come really handy for creating very detailed designed candles.

Some people say that you should not use spray on these molds, but I can't fully agree. I had situations when I couldn't take the candles out. After a couple of these events, I stopped making candles with silicone molds without using release spray. But it's just a preference, so you should test and see how it works for you.

The only thing that you should keep in mind is that silicone molds are very popular due to their great results. Yet, they are also more expensive than other versions. The good news is that if you buy such a mold and take good care of it, you will have it for a very long time.

DIY Candle Molds

The great thing about candle molds is that you can actually find inspiration wherever you look. With just a little bit of imagination, you can use almost anything as a mold. Well, of course, as you already know, the 'mold' has to be heatproof, won't crack, and won't leak.

Let me give you just an example of items I like to use. My favorite DIY mold is probably an eggshell, yet, I also love seashells. As you see, both examples are very easily found in any house, and they are just a mere illustration of how easy it is to let your imagination go wild.

Now, as popular molds are in the candle-making business, I need to tell you that you can also work without them. And no, I am not talking about containers. I am talking about creating hand-dipped candles without any kind of mold. So let me tell you exactly what I am talking about.

Hand-Dipped Candles Without Molds

I have to say right from the start that not everybody is made for this kind of crafting. At least, not at the beginning. Yet, this technique is as old as colonial times.

But what does this method mean? How can you create a candle with no mold or container?

Long story short, you will have to dip the wick in the wax multiple times. So what you do is pour the melted wax into a large pot, then dip the wick repeatedly in the wax until the resin accumulates more and more around the wick. You stop when you reach the diameter you want.

Even though it sounds like an easy task, I will highlight again that this kind of crafting requires some skills and practice. Another thing that you should know is that no matter how many years of experience you have, hand-dipped candles will always look a little bit bumpy and won't be as smooth as molded candles. However, remember that many people like to see the touch of hand-made on their products, so it might actually be a good thing.

Either way, my advice is to understand your customers and their preferences before you start campaigning with these candles.

Now, I hate to be the one to give you the news, but buying just the wax, wicks, dye, fragrance, and mold won't make you a candle-crafter. No. You'll have to make other investments at the beginning of the road. Of course, many of them are a one-time expense, but you should be aware of their importance and don't find yourself in the impossibility of finishing your project.

This being said, let's take a peek at the last part of this very long chapter.

Additional Tools

I don't know about you, but I literally hate those twisted ways of presenting the requirements for when you start a business. I know that most of them are based on their importance, but I do believe that after reading such a list, you are only left with a head-spinning. Again, it might just be me, but when this happens, I usually end up forgetting everything and need to start over and create my own list. Yes, I love my lists.

Anyway, long story short, I will present the equipment based on their use and not by any other fancy, academic way other people like to present them.

Measuring Instruments

When talking about measuring instruments, you will depend on two main categories - digital scale and thermometers.

In the making candle business, instruments for measuring are essential to achieve the best results. Truth be told, I can't see how you could work without having a digital scale, and I will tell you exactly why.

First of all, you will manage to use the exact same quantity of material each time. Because, yes, you already know that you have to write them down whenever you reach that perfect recipe.

You might wonder why I specifically highlighted that the scale must be a digital one. I actually had this kind of talk with other fellow colleagues of mine who said that any accurate scale could handle the business. I couldn't contradict them because they have a point. But if you want to be a professional and not just another fair crafter, you want to follow by the latter your recipe. And that can only be done with a digital scale as it is the only precise method.

The best thing about them is that we have reached the point in time when these scales are pretty inexpensive, and you can find one in every general store.

As a matter of fact, a brushed stainless-steel platform is ideal for precisely weighing the wax, especially when making small candles. Furthermore, stainless steel is easy to clean. This means that even if you spill some wax, there is no problem solving the issue.

The last piece of advice I can give you on the matter of digital scales is this: always use the same unit conversion. Pick one and be consistent. I personally like to work in grams but feel free to choose your own favorite.

So scales are to establish weight, but heat is just as important when making candles. And that's why thermometers are vital for your business.

Without too many intros and explanations, a digital thermometer will do exactly what you think - they instantly read temperature characteristics, letting you know if the wax has been adequately heated.

As a piece of advice, you can even use kitchen thermometers. Yes, they are acceptable for cooking; therefore, they are great for checking the temperature of oil and water, as well as wax.

As a matter of fact, one of the most significant advantages of using a cooking thermometer is that you can straightforwardly wash them under running water as soon as you finish the work.

If you are wondering which type of kitchen thermometer you should choose, I can tell you that there are three models that are perfectly suited for candle making. You can try them all and decide which one you find handier.

The first natural choice might be a digital thermometer. Such an item is durable, convenient, and precise. You can very easily read the temperature on display and most probably can choose if you want to work in Fahrenheit or Celsius.

The next option would be a candy thermometer. This one is a bare glass tool that has been a dominant option in candlemaking for decades. They can handle really high temperatures, making them very suitable for candle crafting.

Finally, you can go with a model that is a little bit more expensive than the other ones. Known as dial thermometers, these designs are less fragile, more durable, and timeless.

<u>Wick Setting Tools</u>

Next on the list of pieces of equipment, you cannot miss wick setting accessories. As their name implies, these tools make sure that the wick stays perfectly in the center of your jar or any other container you might use. I really love working with these items because they automatically center and set the wick by precise measurements. You literally don't need to spend a lot of time and energy using it as it suits even the most extensive possible container sizes.

The innovative design comes with six particular diameters, allowing you to use the tool for multiple sizes. The best part? It takes a few seconds to adjust it from one jar to another. Of course, there are tens of different container sizes nowadays, and the wick setting tool might not hold all of them. Luckily, in many cases, you can send the device back to the manufacturer, and they will modify and send it back to you.

In addition to the wick setting tool, you will need to use some glue dots that keep the wick fixed on the bottom of the container but also some bow tie wick bar for centering the wick on the wax surface.

I wouldn't skip any of these three elements as they will be a great addition to your final work, helping you create a complex system for centering the wicks with precision.

<u>Pouring Pot</u>

A pouring pot is also an essential component of the candle-making complete kit. Such an item is usually made of aluminum. It is about 3 quarts and can hold up to 4 pounds of wax.

Now, the way I like to work is to use different pouring pots for each candle fragrance I produce. However, this tactic is not necessary for beginners. Until you familiarize yourself with pouring pots, I suggest sticking just to one. Luckily, most of the candle-making starter kits include a mini pouring pot. Therefore you can make yourself comfortable with its way of working.

<u>Extra Equipment To Ease Your Work</u>

All the items I told you about are a must. But that is just my opinion, of course. Other crafters might tell you otherwise. Anyway, you should know that if you are in this business for long enough, you will end up using some other helping items. Most likely, you will find some of these ideas totally useless while others will be life-changing. Here is how my shopping list looks when I want to upgrade my supplies in no actual order.

- Pipettes for accurately measuring

- Disposable gloves

- Extension cords or power boards

- Fire blankets

- Fire extinguishers

- Table covers (aluminum or wax sheets)

- Stirring spoons (ideally plastic ones, as wood spoons would absorb perfume and color)

- Wick sizing templates

- Paper towels and cloths

- Metal scoops for wax

- Bucket for collecting waste

- Wick trimmers (nail trimmers or scissors)

Yeah, I told you I have a list for everything. And we are just at the 4th chapter of this journey.

Packaging supplies

Last but not least, you should consider the packing supplies you need. Carton boxes are the most common ones and should be the same size as the candle.

As a piece of advice, I can only tell you to choose vertically square boxes to suit extra packaging, mainly transporting glass jar candles.

Let's recap for a second. You have your wax, and you have your wicks, your colors, and your molds. You even have additional tools to help you along the way. But how can you have the best results if you don't do the proper work setup?

I must admit that I am a mess when it comes to getting organized. I always liked to say that I prefer working in my original tidy mess. However, when I started to produce candles to sell, I realized that my way of working was no longer an option. So I had to learn how to do a proper workspace setup.

Now, I don't know if you are as messy as me. Most probably, you're not. However, I cannot move further without telling you what I learned in the last couple of years so you won't find yourself as lost as me.

Without no further ado, here's how to set up your candle-making workspace.

How To Set Up Your Candle-Making Workspace

Whether candle-making is only a hobby or your intention is to transform it into a business, it is essential to plan a perfectly set up workspace. You need good lighting (natural if possible), a well-ventilated space, as well as comfortable conditions to work in.

Working with wax needs an environment that is neither too hot nor cold; otherwise, the final product may lack quality. Here are the professional recommendations for setting up the workspace, along with some additional equipment you need.

The good thing about starting the candle crafting setup is that most of the necessary items are already in your possession. For instance, make your workbench out of any comfortable workbench you have around.

If you prefer using a usual kitchen bench, make sure you lay at least a towel to avoid the jars getting cold.

Place it in an area you have or can place some shelves. They will be perfect for storing supplies and equipment at a hand's reach. Now, if you can have a sink nearby, it's even better. It's not mandatory, but I find this setup to be very useful.

Speaking of sinks, you should never pour the wax into the drain. If you constantly do so, you risk clogging down your drain. And you know that can only mean that you will need to hire a plumber and waste some workdays. Yes, this is one of the most costly mistakes. My simple advice is to keep a bucket on hand for wax waste and water. And by the way, soy wax is biodegradable, making it kind of safe to pour it into the garden once it cools down.

So having a sink is not mandatory, but having a power source around your workbench is. You will need it for a lot of your electrical supplies because having extension cords all over your house is no fun. Oh, and speaking of electrical power, you should consider having a microwave around.

Finally, try spreading aluminum foil or wax paper on the working desk to level up your cleaning process. This way, you will easily peel off the spilled wax. Trust me on this! Been there, done that without the foil, and it's not a fun activity.

And with this, we wrap up the topic of candle-making equipment. I am well aware that it was a super long chapter, and there is a lot to take in. So, if you want to take a break and digest everything you just read, it's totally understandable. I know exactly how you feel. I was you, remember?

Anyway, we will continue our learning and discovering journey with another fun chapter whenever you are ready. This being said, I will move on and wait for you whenever you are ready to continue.

Chapter Five

The Making Process

H ey, you! So good to see you again. How are you doing? I hope I didn't lose you on the way and that you understood everything I've explained so far. I have prepared for you a FAQ chapter that will probably share more light on all manners presented in this book.

But we have much more to discuss until that point. We will talk about marketing strategies, finding markets, shipping methods, and all that jazz. So the questions will pile up. I have no doubt about that. However, now it's not the time for any of that. Now is the time to discuss how we actually make candles.

But until then, I want to talk a little bit about some safety measures you will have to take when crafting candles.

Safety measures

If you are at this point of the book, you most certainly are aware that crafting candles is not just a means to an end but also a relaxing way to express yourself. Furthermore, you most probably are aware of the fact that since you will be literally playing with fire, you need to take some precautions. And truth be told, it doesn't matter how much experience you have, you always need to be careful and make sure that no accidents happen while working.

Technically speaking, there aren't too many things you need to look out for. I mean, it's not like you are splitting an atom. But you are going to maneuver hot wax. And when combined with a fire source, it can mean some nasty burns. Anyway, I am sure that you already know most of the advice I am about to give you. Yet, regardless of your level of knowledge, I will tell you how I like to work to avoid any injuries. Better to bore you with the obvious than to feel bad that I didn't warn you.

The first thing that I make sure of when I work is that I have safety equipment on hand. But what does that mean? It means that I use potholders when handling pans. Also, I sometimes even use safety goggles when I pour the wax into my molds. I have to admit that this is not something I do very often now, but I didn't work without them at the beginning. When you are at the beginning of the road, you tend to splash hot wax, and you definitely don't want it in your eyes.

Another thing that makes me work more relaxed is having a fire extinguisher around. I have to admit that I never used it, but since hot wax is very similar to hot oil, let's just say that I work with more confidence with a fire extinguisher by my side.

Oh, and also, it is wise to have a first aid kit in proximity. You never know when you need it.

Another piece of advice I can't give you enough is only to use proper candle crafting equipment. I know that I already told you about the tools you should use, but I want to highlight that each of them is very important. Moreover, I have to advise you not to use the cheapest equipment possible. I know that when you are at the beginning of the road, you may be tempted not to invest too much. But high-quality tools can really make the difference not only when it comes to the final result but also for your safety.

The next thing I will tell you is probably more than obvious, but you should not think that this is something you should ignore. I don't know how you live or where you plan to work, but you should be very careful if you have kids or pets around.

Of course, many projects are perfectly safe to do with children, but even so, they require many precautions. The idea is simple. No matter how well-behaved kids and pets are, they should never be left without constant supervision when working with hot wax, knives, or other sharp or hot objects.

Not only can they hurt themselves very badly, but they can also destroy your working environment. This takes me to the next recommendation, which is - always keep your things tidy.

Always make sure that you keep a clean workspace. The last thing you want is to work with fire around flammable objects. Remember how I told you about the fire extinguisher? Well, try to keep it as much as possible as a decorative item.

Well, I guess this is basically it. I mean, of course, you should take care of your hair and clothes. But other than that, you should be safe.

With the safety measures out of the way, we can now focus on the actual manufacturing processes.

If you are a candle enthusiast, you don't need me to tell you that there is more than one type of candle out there. And I don't mean waxes. I mean about actual candle shapes and sizes. Because of their great variety, I want to take a walk around them understand their characteristics and the best way to use them.

Tealight Candles

The first model I want to talk about is the small and delicate tealight candle. Also known as a tea candle, this example is small and circular, often placed in a thin metal cup. Their name is very straightforward as these candles are usually used in teapot warmers.

Due to their low price, tea candles are very popular, especially for heating scented oil or accent lighting. However, my favorite way to use tealight candles is to place them on water. Thanks to their floating properties and also the fact that they don't drip, they can create beautiful decorative effects.

Now, remember my grandmother and her beeswax candles? Well, those were not the only ones that she burned. I told you that she was superstitious, but I failed to say that she was also religious. Each Sunday morning, she lit such a candle in her kitchen and said a prayer over it. Naturally, since I was a curious kid, I asked why did she use different candles for each of her activities. She was a simple woman who didn't use too many words. So she didn't basically explain anything but said that the tealight candles are for religious purposes, and that was it.

Later on, I understood that they were safe to burn due to their tin container. Furthermore, since they don't drip, they didn't pose a threat to her small "kitchen altar."

Anyway, let's leave granny aside for a while as I am sure that I will find more stories about her to tell you. Instead of talking about my childhood, I want to get back to the tealight characteristics. So, I told you that these candles are small and round. But how small? Well, there are two very popular sizes you should know about. There is the bigger version of 1.5in diameter, and then there is the smaller one of 0.63 in diameter.

Regarding the wax type used for crafting such candles, these candles are often made with white unscented resin. Therefore, if you think about producing these candles, you should consider either paraffin or soy wax. As for the wick, you should make sure that you anchor it well to prevent floating to the top of the molted wax. The reason why you need to make sure this doesn't happen is that you don't want the wick to burn out before the wax does.

When testing your candles to see if you can produce a clean-burning, keep in mind that tealight candles burn for about 3 hours. Yet, if you burn more than one at the same time, they will tend to burn faster due to bigger oxygen consumption. Understood? Fantastic! Now, let's see exactly how to craft tealight candles.

Crafting Steps

I am sure that each crafter has its own way of producing candles. So please understand that what I am about to tell you is just to have a reference point. As you will evolve, you will most probably discover your own approaches and work styles. But until then, here is how I like to perform my business.

Regardless of the next steps, the first thing you need to do is to measure and melt your wax. When making tealight candles, you can't make just one. I mean, you could, but that is a waste of time and resources. Anyway, I suggest you start working in 10-candle batches. After mastering such a batch, it is very easy to multiply the number.

This being said, for a 10-candle batch, you will need 200g of wax. Measure it with your digital scale as you want to be 100% precise. Place the wax in a heat-proof container and melt it using either a stove or a microwave. This part is strictly up to you.

Anyway, remember how I said that you need to really anchor the wick for tealight candles? Well, you will need to use some glue dots for this. Don't worry as it's not a hard task. You will have to stick the glue dots to the bottom of the wicks, then place the wicks right in the middle of your container. Again, don't worry because you can't miss the center. The containers have a middle mark so that you won't have to decide on your own.

With the help of your wick setting tool, hold the wicks in place, then prepare the wax. As I said, tealight candles are usually white and odorless. However, if you want to make them colorful, you can do that. Just wait for the melted wax to cool down a little. You want it to be around 150 Fahrenheit. Add the dye, following the instructions, then gently stir until the color has completely blended into the wax.

Furthermore, after coloring the wax, you can also add a fragrance if you want to make the candles more festive. For 200g of wax, you should not go beyond 10ml of fragrance oil. But again, you should trust the manufacturer's instructions. After adding the oil, stir once more to have a homogeneous mixture.

And now you are ready to pour the wax!

Before you start pouring the wax into the containers, you need to make sure that it is at the right temperature. You want it to be somewhere between 120 and 140 Fahrenheit. If your wax is within those limits, carefully pour it into the prepared containers and let it sit at least overnight at room temperature. However, I do advise you not to rush the process and wait for 24 hours.

The final step you will need to take is to trim the wicks. So, the next day, after the wax is all stable and nice, take the wick centering tools off and get ready to trim your wicks. I don't go further than 5mm. I find this number to be the most appropriate for my work, but again, please test and find your own path.

Votive Candles

Votive candles are a fantastic way to upgrade a room's design by offering a cozy ambiance. What I love about votives is their versatility since they can easily be used in any room as well as outside. Let me tell you in a few words exactly what I mean.

Imagine this - you can light votives on your dining table, dim the lights and create a romantic atmosphere. Furthermore, if you are that kind of lucky person who has a fireplace, you can place some votives on it and give the room a Christmasy feeling any time you like. The best thing about setting the mood with votives is their subtle and intimate way of burning. They make their presence noticeable but don't take all the attention on the room.

These candles are also small yet slightly bigger than tealight candles. However, many people confuse the two, and they are not to blame. But let's talk a little bit about the votives' features. I am sure that after that, you won't have any problem differentiating them.

So you already know that tealight candles come in their own containers, and that is probably one of the biggest differences between the two. Because votives are independent candles with no container, therefore, they need specific support to be used. I've seen many crafters sell a votive-like kit in the last few years. What this means is that they sell a votive that is pre-poured into a container, plus one or two refills. Actually, this is a very nice way to offer your clients beautiful votive supports without charging them extra.

The most popular containers for votives are made out of glass, and I strongly believe that they are indeed an elegant choice as well as a timeless one. It really doesn't matter if we talk about a modern apartment or a cozy cabin; glass votive containers find their way in every house.

You can choose to market your votives in colorful, frosted, speckled, or tarnished glass holders. Yet, for me, the classical containers are the best.

Plus, they are super easy to clean. Oh, and as a suggestion, if you decide to sell votive kits, give your clients instructions on how to handle the container before they use it for the refill. Not a necessary step, but an appreciated one nevertheless.

But let's move on and talk a little more about the actual votives. So, these candles come in different heights, and since they are bigger by all means than tealight candles, votives have a better burn time. Even so, they will reach a moment when the flame simply burns out, and you need to replace the candle. Yet, since votives burn in holders, you will need to clean the container before replacing the candle. And that is why I suggested that you explain this 'sanitization' part to your clients.

Now, regarding the wax choice, you can make votives basically using any resin you want, but the most popular choices are paraffin, beeswax, and soy.

Up until I started to craft candles, I was sure that votives were just white and odorless. But that's not true. I mean, yes, most often than not, this is how you'll find votives, but you can use dyes and fragrances.

However, most votive candles are without any kind of fragrance because they are very popular to be used as dining table decor. I mean, when you enjoy a nice dinner, you don't want a fragrance to intervene with whatever you are eating. Imagine having a delicious stew or pasta. You definitely don't want the smell of vanilla or pumpkin to envelop the room.

Yet, that doesn't mean that fragranced votives don't have their place in the world. For instance, I love to use these candles when I take one of those long and relaxing bubble baths. Placing fragrant votives on my tub makes me relax, giving me a spa sensation. And I am sure that I am not the only one who loves doing this.

Anyway, let's not linger too long on the topic of what I like and what I don't. Better yet, let me give you a few tips and tricks for making the most beautiful votive candles.

Crafting Steps

I know that we are only at the second type of candle, but you need to know that I will explicitly say when you have to measure your wax each time.

Many people think to work guided by instinct, but that should not be you. You want to be precise, remember?

So, the first thing you need to do in order to craft votives is to choose your wax and weigh it. Depending on how big you want your candles to be, you will manage to create somewhere around 8 and 10 votives from a pound of wax.

As you will see, votive wax will need some cutting, and that can be a little tricky. I suggest you use a utility knife and score the wax using it. The next step is to place the scored piece on the remaining slab then apply pressure to help the wax break on the score. If you don't succeed from the first try, don't worry. You simply may need to repeat the process to break the wax into small parts to fit in the pouring pot.

The only piece of advice I can give you at this point is to be careful how you handle the knife and weigh your wax directly in the pouring pot. I imagine that I don't have to explain the very obvious reasons for these suggestions. Therefore I will move on.

So, once you have all the wax you need, you can start melting it. Heat the wax until you reach a temperature between 175 and 185 Fahrenheit. Basically, the temperature difference is given by the wax you choose.

Anyway, I like to melt my wax using a double boiler in this specific case. If you have any pastry-making experience, then you know what I am talking about. This technique, which allows you to make the delicious vanilla egg custard, is also very useful for melting wax.

Basically, what you have to do is to take a saucepan and fill it with about an inch of water. Place it on the stove and heat it up. Ideally, this pan will allow you to put the pouring pot on top of it and melt the wax thanks to the steam without the pot touching the boiling water. But if you can't find such a pan, just make sure the heat is set to low. You want the wax to melt without receiving direct heat.

While you wait for the wax to melt, stir continuously, and don't forget to check the temperature. After you gain enough experience, you can prepare the wicks while the wax is melting, but I don't recommend you to do this right from the start.

Anyway, after you finish melting your wax, let it sit at a stable temperature and move your focus on the molds.

Number one tip on the matter: always work with clean molds. Truth be told, even when they are brand new, mold still needs to be cleaned. Many of them come with a layer of oil, and if you don't remove it, you won't get the best results.

The best way to attack the problem is to use a mild cleaner, a paper towel, and your cleaning charms. I mean it. It's that simple. You pour a little bit of cleaner on the paper towel, then use it to wipe the inside of the mold.

Now, I know that many people say that cooking spray is just as good, but I can't stand beside this approach. But, just as always, please test and decide for yourself.

If you choose to work with auto-wick pins, this is the moment when you want to set them inside the votive molds. If you have regular wicks, then skip this step and prepare your molds in such a way that will allow you to pour the wax easily. I like to place them in a single row, but you do your own magic.

Again, the next steps are optional. If you want to create white and odorless candles, then you should not be interested in what I am about to say. But if you are, then be careful.

With the wax at the discussed temperature, you can add the fragrance you wish. In theory, 1 ounce of fragrance oil is enough for one pound of wax. But, be sure to read the manufacturer's instructions and follow your previous measurements.

Regardless of how much oil you use, transfer it to the melted wax and stir for about 2-3 minutes to give the wax time to absorb the fragrance completely.

Once this is done, you can focus on the color part. This part is a little bit different based on the type of dye you use. For instance, if you are using blocks, simply measure it as instructed, cut it into small pieces, then melt it into the wax. Sir everything to ensure a perfect blend.

If you prefer using liquid dye, then it's even easier. You just transfer the desired amount of drops right on top of the wax. Stir after each addition and wait to see the result. The last thing you want is to ruin your work due to an undesirable color.

Now regardless of the type of dye you choose to use, you should remember that when it's hot, the wax has a darker color than when it's cooled. This is why I strongly recommend testing the color before calling it a wrap.

Drip a small amount of wax on a paper towel and let it cool. If you still think it needs more color after a couple of minutes, then add more color. But it's better to be 100% sure.

This next part is also optional. Some crafters say it's a must, but others say it's just a myth. I personally have mixed feelings about this topic - adding UV stabilizers.

This will help you stabilize the color if your candles are exposed to UV rays. I never use such a component for white candles, and since I like my votives white and odorless, I don't see its use. However, if you wish to create vibrant colors for your votives, make sure to use about half a teaspoon of stabilizer at a pound of wax.

Transfer it to the hot wax and stir until it is perfectly dissolved.

Great!

We are finally at a point where it's mandatory for all votive crafters, and that is pouring the wax mixture. Therefore, pour the wax mixture into your prepared molds. Take your time when pouring. By hurrying the process, your wax can create bubbles at the top of the wax, and you most definitely don't want that.

If you used votive wick pins, then fill the molds. Let the candles cool completely before taking further action.

But if you use normal wicks, leave a few free millimeters when pouring the wax. Keep the remaining wax in the pouring pot as you will need it to finish the candles.

So I will assume that you are using normal wicks just for the sake of the conversation. If this is the case, check the wicks to see if they are straight. If you see them curling, then gently use your fingers to straighten them.

With this out of the way, it's time to insert the wicks in the wax. However, I suggest you wait for the wax to set around the edges before taking any action. When ready, cut through the top of the wax with the wick, inserting it in each mold. Center the wicks, making sure that they are perfectly anchored. It should feel as if the wick's tab is stuck at the bottom of the mold.

With this done, we are back to the same point as when using votive wick pins. Therefore, you can let your candles cool down completely. I prefer to let them rest for at least 8 hours, but you could continue in just a couple of hours.

Anyway, when the wax is completely cooled, you will notice a sinkhole that appears due to wax shrinking. This is why I told you to keep the remaining wax in the pouring pot. You will need it to finish the candles. So, you will have to re-melt the wax, but this time raise the temperature even higher. Why? Because the hotter the temperature your wax has at the second pour, the better will the two layers will blend. I would suggest going to 190 Fahrenheit, but if you reach 200 is just as fine.

At this time, you will need to let the wax cool completely. Don't even think about rushing the process. If the candles are not perfectly cooled, the wax may spill over the mold's sides.

But if the wax is completely set, you can indeed remove the votives from their molds. This should be a very easy task. Just pull the wick, and the candle should come out easily. However, if you see that the situation doesn't go as smoothly as I say, you can place the molds for 5 minutes in the freezer. This should help you finish the task. Yet, don't forget the molds in the freezer, or you will end up with cracked candles.

If you've used wick pins, remove them by holding the candle in one hand and tapping the pin against any hard surface. Doing so will help the pin to slide out the bottom, giving you the chance to pull it out.

Finally, regardless of the wicks you've used, it's time to trim them. You should trim them no more than 1/4 inch in length because they will end up burning unproperly. You can use any item you feel more comfortable with for this task. I prefer wick trimmers, but you can also go with nail clippers or scissors.

Pillars

I don't know about you, but I absolutely love pillar candles. I don't know why, but I always found them to be extremely elegant. This feeling is probably given by their chic widebodies and their lovely way of spreading light when burning. With this introduction out of the way, let's talk about what pillars are, their features, and, of course, how to craft them.

So, pillars are candles that can burn for an extended period of time due to their increased amount of wax to fuel the flame. Actually, a pillar can burn for almost 60 hours, which is quite impressive, I might say. Therefore, they are very pretty items and very practical ones to have around the house.

I hope that you don't mind but I want to linger a little bit more on the topic of burning time as I do believe it is very important to understand that are many aspects that can influence it. As you probably imagine, the main aspects that have a thing to say on the matter are the size and the components. There's no doubt that high-quality candles burn clean, but they do it for a longer time.

Yet, there are a few tricks you can take out your sleeves to make pillars burn more effectively, tricks that I suggest you also share with your customers.

For instance, one thing that always works is to make sure that the wick is always trimmed to ¼". I know that it may sound like too much of a hassle, but removing any wick trimmings before lighting really makes the difference. Furthermore, the first burn is crucial regardless of what others tell you. The best advice I can give regarding this part is to let the candle burn for one hour for each diameter inch. After that, you should extinguish the flame and allow it to cool completely.

By advising your customers to act this way, you will not only increase the quality of your products but also their trust in you.

Anyway, let's move on to the point in which I tell you that these candles can be burned in more than a different way. Even so, I always suggest using a candleholder as it reduces the risk of fire. I know that many people burn pillar candles on plates and trays, but I can't support this. What a candleholder does is catch the wax and stabilize the candle, giving you an extra safety layer.

Now speaking of wax, just like other models, pillars can also be crafted from more than one type of resin. Yet, I do believe that a rigid wax is the best in this case. Naturally, I can only talk about my preferences on the matter, but I do prefer working mostly with paraffin and beeswax for manufacturing pillars.

So, without further ado, let me guide you through the process of crafting pillars.

Crafting Steps

Since this is the third type of candle we are talking about, I will try to only refer to the steps that we've already discussed. I don't want to tell you over and over again the same thing. This book needs to be fun, and reading the same thing is anything but fun.

So, choose your wax, score it, cut it and measure it directly in your pouring pot. Using a double boiler, heat the wax and melt it, stirring from time to time and checking the temperature.

Remember what I told you that you should clean your mold even if they are new? This is really important so never forget this part. You won't get the best results if you don't use clean molds. And I assume that since you are reading this book, you want to be a pro and not an amateur. So wash your molds!

Since pillar molds come in different sizes and heights, I can only suggest choosing a wick that is somewhere around 6 inches to the height of your chosen mold. Of course, you can adjust the size based on your preferences but start from this point. After choosing your wick, string it through the hole at the bottom of the mold. You will see that you will be left with a few inches of your wick hanging out. That's normal.

Anyway, it's time to anchor the wick. To do so, just hold it at the bottom of the mold, and with the help of a sticky tack, roll it until you get a ball shape, then press it firmly. But don't rush the process. If you are not careful, you can cause a leaking issue. Just to be 100% sure you don't ruin your work surface, place the mold on a paper plate or something similar.

After finishing with the bottom anchor, it's time to secure the top part of the wick. How can you do this? Well, very simple, actually. You just pull the wick tight, so there is no slack in it, then slide it into the slot in the wick bar.

Now it's all about preparing the wax. If you want to color it or make it smell in a specific way, you know the steps. Basically, follow the instructions given by the manufacturer, and you should be more than fine.

The only part I want to highlight again is that you should test your color before declaring yourself satisfied.

So once you have all your components mixed, it is time to take your pouring pot away from the heat and pour the wax into your prepared molds. Don't rush the process as you don't bubble to form at the top of your wax. Pour the wax until you reach the top level of the mold. This will be your first pour, so don't worry about the remaining wax from your pouring pot. That is for the final pour.

You will see that slowly, your wax will start to set, and with this, you will need to help it release the air pockets that naturally occur with the cooling and shrinking of your wax. To do so, you will need to make something called 'relief holes.'

Using a skewer, poke tiny holes whenever you see a film-like skin forming across the wax. The only thing that you need to be careful about is to make the pokes in such a way that they are deep into the candle but don't hit the side of the mold. If this happens, you will scar your candle, and I assume that you don't want to do that.

After taking care of this part, it's time to let your wax cool down and prepare yourself for the second pouring. Again, don't rush the process. Let the wax cool completely before pouring the final part of wax. When you are ready to finish the batch, heat up the wax once more and pour your second level of wax. Be sure not to go past the first pour line, or else you will notice an edge on your candles.

Now, all you have to do is wait for the wax to cool completely and remove the candles from the molds. As previously said, leave your wax to completely cool for 24 hours, remove the anchors from the bottom of the mold and get the candles out.

If you cleaned the molds properly and worked properly, you should not have any problems taking the candles out. But if you do, you already know my advice. Just place the molds in the freezer for a while. All right?

Taper Candles

I can't say for a fact, but I am almost certain that the first candle I ever saw was a taper. I mean, most probably, I've stumbled upon birthday candles, but I can't remember them.

Anyway, now we are talking about tapers, so let's not go too deep into my childhood memories.

The point of my introduction is to highlight the fact that I have no doubt that everyone has seen taper candles at least more than one time. Even if you think that you don't know them, once you finish reading what I have to say about them, you will most certainly realize that you've known these candles all along.

So tapers have a long and slim aspect, making them perfect for romantic dinner tables as well as very modern spaces. In other words, a taper is the best item that can decorate any antique furniture but also a cutting-edge modern table.

Even though tapers find their way in any room of a house, due to their appearance, they are best suited for areas of focus and, of course, dinner tables.

The beautiful thing about tapers is that they really are the types of candles that are appropriate in any color. However, since they are very suitable for dinner tables, I don't really recommend adding any fragrance to them.

I bet that by now, you most certainly know what type of candles I am talking about, yet you most probably don't know that this model is actually one of the oldest ones. Yes, that's right. They go all the way back to the first history page.

The good thing about the evolution of tapers is that today they can be crafted using the best high-quality wax and can burn clean. Speaking of wax, one of the best indicators of the wax's quality when it comes to tapers is the side dripping. The reason for the dripping is actually the wax. Simply put - the looser the wax, the bigger the mess.

Now let me tell you a secret. A while ago, a customer of mine contacted me and asked me if there is such a thing as a dripless taper. As you could probably guess by now, I am an honest person, so I couldn't tell her anything other than the truth. And what that truth might be? Well, even the most high-quality tapers can't be 100% dripless. Yeah. That's the harsh truth. However, there are a few precautions that can be taken to prevent dripping, and I will tell you exactly what I told her.

So tapers are tall and thin, right? Due to their beautiful and elegant appearance, they are actually very easy to position in such a way that they don't stand 100% straight. And due to the beautiful thing called gravity and the wonders of physics, such a burning candle will much more likely spill wax compared to a candle that is majestically straight in its holder.

The logical question in these conditions is how to make sure that your taper doesn't bend. Right?

Well, there are some soft wax disks that can fasten the candles firmly to their holders. Using them will reduce the risk of bending and, therefore, of dripping.

Since we've talked about gravity, I think that it's only natural that we also talk about tapers' height. I mean, it is a very important factor. Now, truth be told, there is no standard when it comes to how tall a taper can be. You will find them anywhere between 6 and 20 inches. I am sure that once you start crafting these candles, you will very soon discover a size that suits your personality and make it your own. For example, I feel very comfortable working with 12 inches molds. They are easy to manufacture and can burn for almost 10 hours. So, yeah, for me, these candles just feel right. But let's see the exact steps to take in order to create these lovely candles.

Crafting Steps

By now, you should already call yourself a crafter. You know the basics of crafting candles. All you have to do is to learn the tricks of creating each model and find your own technique. Thus, these steps are just to give you a start and help you find your path. Therefore, if you feel like something is missing is probably because I already explained it to you. So, naturally, I don't want to repeat myself. With this out of the way, let's take a look at the process of making tapers.

So, prepare your double boiler, measure your wax, cut it and place it in the pouring pot. Melt it and combine it with the dye and fragrance you want. All these are old news by now. Therefore, let's move to more interesting parts.

Tapers can be made with or without using molds. For perfect-looking candles, just use the molds you like, clean them and follow the rules you already know.

However, if you want to really make them stand out, you craft tapers by hand-dipping into the wax. This is actually a very easy project.

Start by choosing the wick you want to work with but make sure that it's long enough. You will have to trim it and also leave at least 2cm extra to be lit when the candle is finished.

Anyway, with the wick trimmed and ready, you can proceed with the next part. Take each wick and carefully submerge it in the hot wax. You will see air bubbles appear. That's normal. Make sure that the wick is covered in wax, take it out and straighten it using your hand. Let it rest and repeat the process with all your wicks.

Some claim that you can make the second dip immediately, but I like to be extra careful. That's why I recommend you wait before you repeat the process and submerge your wicks once more. You can even reduce the wax's temperature for a better build-up.

After the second coating, let the wicks dry completely on a wire rack. From this point forward, you will have to dip the wick and let it dry as many times you want from this point forward. It all depends on how thick you wish your tapers to be. When you reach the desired thickness, just allow your candles to dry for at least 12 hours. When ready, simply cut the wick to the desired length and straighten off the base of your candles with a knife.

As for the wax choice, I love to make beeswax tapers. However, you can also use soy wax or paraffin just as well.

Gel candles

It is my firm belief that you should first master working with hard waxes before you start even considering moving on to crafting gel candles. The technique is not very easy to explain, and simply reading the steps from a manual book won't do it.

It's not that I don't want to teach you. It's just a lot to take in, especially at the beginning of the road. You need to consider many chemical aspects before crafting gel candles. You will need to understand the viscosity of each density gel. You will need to recognize non-polar scents and so on.

Crafting gel candles is not rocket science, and once you get ahold of the technique, it is actually straightforward. But it's very easy to confuse the notions, and that can end up very badly. So, what I want you to remember at this point is that gel candles exist, they require a special kind of attention, and you need experience before you start learning how each component works. All right?

Essential Oils

You may be surprised to realize how much essential oil you need to use in order to get even the faintest aroma while making candles with them. When using essential oils, I only use about 100 drops per pound of wax.

The more you use, the more powerful the aroma will be, but essential oils can also be quite pleasant. However, remember that they are expensive, so don't go overboard. I've included a few additional suggestions in the following paragraphs that may be useful to you. I hope that they will help you save a little money while also refine your candles' fragrance.

Essential Oil Tips

#1: Save money by using generic essential oils. I propose spending the least amount of money possible on the essential oils you'll be using in your candles. For pure essential oils, you can go a little generic here (think oils you might get at your local supermarket or drugstore). It's also worth checking out Plant Therapy's extensive collection of essential oils, which rivals generic products in price but offers superior choice and quality.

#2. Use essential oils to coat your wicks. The first step is to combine some of the essential oils you'll be working with in a shallow dish or tray. Drag your wicks through the oil to allow the wicks to absorb the oils.

Let the wicks air dry on a piece of paper towel or parchment paper. If you're using unwaxed cotton wicking that you intend to wax yourself, it works best, but you may also use pre-waxed ready-made wicks if that's what you have.

#3. A paper towel dipped in essential oil can be used to apply a gentle layer of aroma over the top of a freshly poured candle after it has set and dried. You'll be able to smell it better before you burn it this way and get a better start on the scent.

My Favourite Blends of Essential Oils

When it comes to creating your personalized candle scents, the versatility of essential oils is unmatched. You can mix and match as many oils as you wish. Keep things simple. I usually mix two or three of my own singles together to create a unique scent for myself. Some of my favorites are as follows:

1- Lemon & Lavender

This is a lovely combination for a spring or summer candle or to give as a present for a birthday or Mother's Day. It's bright, fresh, and floral. Lemon and lavender can be mixed together in equal quantities, or three parts lavender and one part lemon if you prefer one scent over the other. The ratio of lemon to lavender and a fifth of another oil is what I use when adding a third scent. Bergamot oil is an optional extra.

2- Black Spruce & Rosemary

This woodsy and earthy blend is ideal for the outdoor enthusiast or the man in your life. This is a wonderful present for Father's Day or any other occasion. To make, combine equal parts rosemary and black spruce (or any spruce or pine) oil and shake well to combine. In order to add a third aroma, blend equal amounts of rosemary, spruce and extra oil.

3- Cinnamon & Orange

This combination is very pleasant on a chilly winter's night because it is warm and spicy. An excellent choice for the holidays, whether in the fall or winter. Mix equal amounts of orange and cinnamon bark oil to create the scent. Orange, cinnamon, and an additional oil can be used if desired. Clove oil can be added as an optional ingredient.

4- Eucalyptus with Tea Tree

When you're sick with a cold or flu, or if you're relaxing in your "home spa," this combination is ideal for cleansing and rejuvenating. Make a blend of peppermint and eucalyptus oils using a 1:1 ratio. Add a third aroma by mixing equal parts peppermint, eucalyptus, and another essential oil.

Now that you know what the ABC of crafting candles is, I think that it's time to talk a little bit more about business. As a creative person, this was the hardest part for me. I had no interest in packaging and markets, but I had to learn to handle them. And so will you. You can't be a business person without these notions. Unfortunately, this is the harsh truth - no matter how good of a crafter you are, you have to go that extra mile if you want to own a successful company.

So, because of that, I will dedicate the next chapter to an extremely important part of becoming an entrepreneur. Let's see what it's all about!

Chapter Six

Packaging & shipping

I f I learned one thing the hard way over the last years is that packaging sells. Sometimes it sells better than the actual product. And that makes total sense, especially when you are new on the market.

Think about new products that caught your eye. Why did they? Think for a second. Was the packaging a very important reason why you considered buying that item or not? I mean, when a brand already has a voice, it's easy to make an opinion about it. You check other customers' reviews, testimonials, and so on. But when it's a no-name that wants to find its way to your heart, how do you decide if it's worth spending money on it or not? You are influenced by its packaging more than its ingredients without even realizing it, and I will tell you exactly why.

Let's not talk candles for a second. Let's talk about face cream. Let's think that you are looking for a vegan moisturizer for sensitive skin. You go to the cosmetic aisle and see a lot of brands that you don't know. How do you decide which creams to take in your hand and read the ingredients and specifications? Before even realizing it, you put your hand on the ones that are visually appealing, on the ones that speak to you. Those creams that you take into your hand are the ones that made you think that they are worth it for you to take the time and read their ingredients. The same applies to your candles.

And this is why in this chapter, we won't be talking only about quality but also about the importance of packaging.

So, when talking about packaging candles, the sky is the limit. You can let your creativity run free and create real art. However, making your candles stand out is not the only thing that you should think about. There are also safety measures as well as costs you need to take into account.

Furthermore, you need to understand that some candles are more fragile than others. This means that they need to be wrapped individually. Therefore, having a universal type of packaging in mind is not an option. Yes, that's right. Think about tapers and pillars. They are gentle items, right? They definitely need special treatment, more special than votives, for example. Fragile candles need wax paper and at least two layers of bubble wraps. Also, you need to make the packaging as less frustrating for your customers as possible.

So, yeah, there is a lot to think about, but fear not. Even though it seems like an impossible task, it actually is not, and I will explain everything in as much detail as possible. Let's have a look, shall we?

Packaging Is An Art

I know that most people who decide to start a candle-crafting business are usually creative souls. Yet, not all of them have an eye when it comes to boxes, ribbons, or cards. I know because I am one of those individuals.

Anyway, as I mentioned earlier, mastering the art of packaging can be your advantage or disadvantage. This means that you have to learn how to play your cards right.

At one point in my life, I took a business course where I learned that packaging should represent no more than 10% of the total cost of a product. This was back in the days when I was studying to become something else than a candle crafter. However, when I suddenly found myself in the position of a businesswoman, I had to think of smarter ways to pack my products and reduce that theoretical percentage. I wanted to find a way not only to improve my margin but also to offer a better price for my customers.

So, what I did was to put down the list of resources I needed for each type of candle and see how can I reduce the costs. Of course, I can't tell you how to conduct your business, but I can give you a hint and a direction. My advice is to take each type of candle and understand what you will need for it in terms of packaging.

I will discuss pillars and tapers as a whole. The reason for that is that they are quite similar in terms of packaging. Since we've discussed their features, you already know that these candles don't have any external protection. They are just stand-alone candles. So, carrying them, shipping them, and keeping them safe along the way may be tricky. I mean, the last thing you want is for your clients to receive the candles broken or cracked. And that can happen if your tapers or pillars are poorly packed. Of course, you can decide on your own packaging, but this is the safest way to handle these candles.

The first thing you'll need is wax paper. With its help, you will wrap each pillar or taper, protecting them from debris and dust. The next item you should use is a bubble wrap which you will wrap generously around the candle. The reason? The bubble wrap protects the candles from minor collisions. Once each individual candle is wrapped, you will need to place it in a cardboard box. Finally, to avoid the candles knocking on the box's walls, you should use some kind of foam or wood wool and fill the empty space.

But as I told you, each type of candle needs special attention. So container models such as tealight or votives should be handled a little bit differently.

Let's make a recap. Do you remember what the most common candle containers are? If your answer is glassware and metal, then you are correct. As you probably could deduce, metals are more resistant than other materials. This is why they don't need that much-taking care of. It's enough to place containers in a box with foam or wood wool. But if you use ceramic or glass containers, well, you will need to wrap them in bubble wrap before placing them in the box.

And these are the basics of packaging. But I can't leave you hanging like this. I mean, you could have figured this out by yourself. And that is not why you choose this book. You chose it to teach you things you don't know. Therefore, here are some of my tips and tricks for reducing my packaging costs.

When you order supplies, they come in boxes, right? And in those boxes, you can find things such as foam and packing peanuts. Do you follow me? What I am trying to point out is that it's okay to recycle whatever you can. Not only do you save the planet but also some money.

Furthermore, don't be afraid to get inspired by other packages you get. It's no shame to appreciate the work done by others and understand the reasoning behind their packages. Because let's face it. We are way past the time when truly unique ideas.

Another idea I can help you with is this - personalize each order. People want to feel special so write down a note when you pack their products. This is the best way to help your customers resonate with your brand.

I know that some people even use perfumed potpourri instead of fillers. Well, I am more old-fashioned, and you know how much I love my notes and writings. Anyway, the sky is the limit, and you should take advantage of this and get your clients closer.

Stickers are also a very good way to make your products stand out. They can be fun and easy to use. Plus, they are basically inexpensive. So instead of writing a big instruction plan on each candle, just put a sticker and let the customers know the important stuff, such as fragrance or burning time.

Another tip that I can give you is to be as organized as possible when preparing your shipments. What this means is that you should sort everything out and divide your merchandise and packaging based on the moment you need them on hand. Let me give you an example, so you can better understand what I am talking about.

Let's say that you just received an order for a batch of mixed candles. Place them on your workspace on one of your sides. I always go with the right part, but please feel free to choose the left one. Anyway, leave the middle free as you will need it to store the wrappers, stickers, bows, and whatever you wish to use. Oh, and a pair of scissors. You must have a pair of scissors.

On the opposite side of the table, place the boxes and the fillers you wish to use.

Having everything at hand's reach will allow you to proceed and work almost in a rhythm.

So, working from right to left or from left to right, take one candle at a time and wrap it as I advised you just a little earlier. Add the stickers or ribbons or whatever you want, then place them in a box, filling the gaps with the fillers. Close the box and write down the name and address of your client. With this out of the way, you can move to the next order and keep everything tidy.

A word of advice - when securing the box, use packing tape on both ends. And no, neither regular Scotch nor masking tape is not an option. Why? Because more likely than not, they will not survive the shipping process, and you don't want your customers to contact you for a refund due to delivering them damaged goods.

Another thing I learned the hard way is to never work on more than one order at a time. I did that, and it turned out to be a complete disaster, if you know what I mean.

Anyway, I don't want to get into more details because I am sure that you can imagine that I shipped the wrong merchandise to the wrong clients.

However, I want to give you one last piece of advice regarding the packaging part. Shipping your candles is a little bit tricky during the summer months. Why? Well, naturally, heat is no friend for your waxy products.

This is why you should look for insulating wrappers for hot periods. I like to use air pillows, but sometimes they are simply not enough. So when temperatures hit really high, I also add cold packs to keep the candles cool. Also, even though it costs a little bit more, choose express shipping.

I am aware that this is the second time I am mentioning shipping costs, so it's about time to focus next which is the shipping part. Naturally! Because what good packaging is if your work doesn't reach your customers? Therefore, let's look into this specific part.

How to Ship Your Candles

I know that we haven't talked about marketing strategies, but I can assure you that you will conduct your business online more likely than not. And that is the beauty of living in this era.

Anyway, what I want to ask you is to take this matter as seriously as possible. It can be a total disaster if it's not done right. And yes, I won't lie to you. Shipping candles can be a tricky job.

As you probably imagined, I didn't tell you all about wrapping candles for nothing. No. That part is extremely important because candles only seem sturdy when in fact, they are delicate. And this delicacy can get them damaged if you don't take care of them.

But using fillers and wrappers is not the only part that will ensure your candles have a safe journey to their final owners. There are other things that you need to consider before shipping your merchandise.

One of these factors is weight, and I will explain exactly why that is. Think about glass and tin containers. They are beautiful by all means, right? Of course, they are. But they are also heavier than other candles.

So, even though you wrap your glass vessels as thoroughly as possible to avoid damages, you are still going to face gravity. And yes, you are right. This is not the first time I am bringing physics into the discussion. Anyway, without sounding smart or cocky, the reason why I am highlighting this is that I once used a box that was not fitted to hold the weight I wanted to ship. The result? The box broke, the candles fell on the ground, making me say really bad words.

The only advice I can give you related to this topic is not very professional but more of a matter of preference. I usually choose mailers for pillar and tea candles and more durable corrugated boxes for glass or tin containers.

I told you that it's a great idea to reuse the packages you receive with your own orders. But if your business will be successful, and I do wish you the best of luck with it, you will need more boxes and wrappers.

So just as you find proper suppliers for your manufacturing materials, you will also need to find a proper supplier for your packing materials. This includes everything from boxes to fillers, tape, and tissue paper.

But choosing the right box and the best suppliers is not everything when it comes to delivering your products. Actually, this is just the peak of the iceberg when it comes to shipping your candles. Heavier boxes mean increased costs. And this takes us to the next part of our discussion - the actual shipping.

I know that many of you are terrified by this part. I don't judge you because I know that it might sound like a very hard task, especially if you've never had to deal with such aspects before. But the good news is that it's actually not an impossible task. All you have to do is to do a little bit of planning.

Truth be told, shipping your orders is a repetitive task, and in time you will see it as a daily routine. You know, like washing your teeth or something.

Now, there are many courier companies you could choose from. The most frequently used services are FedEx, UPS, and USPS. But there are others you can consider. Anyway, you should set up an account with one of these guys.

I will go ahead and suppose that you are a US citizen and that most of your shipments will be within the American borders. But if you are located in any other country, you should apply the same patterns but adjust them to your case.

Anyway, a little bit earlier, I told you that weight is a very important aspect when it comes to shipping costs. However, I didn't give you too much information on the matter because I wanted to explain how to calculate your costs in more detail.

So, no matter what country you are from, the cheapest service you can use for shipping your orders is most probably the national postal service. For instance, in the United States, Postal's First Class is the best option if you want to ship packages under one pound. But for shipments over one pound, you should look at the USPS Priority Mail, as I do believe that they offer the most affordable alternatives.

But the weight is not the only part that is going to increase the costs. Even if you are shipping a very lightweight package, you will most probably have to pay more if it's a bulky one. Furthermore, urgent deliveries also increase the total amount the courier company will charge you.

It will take a while for you to learn all tricks to ship the orders at an advantageous price, but until then, you can use the couriers' online calculators. You will have to answer some basic questions regarding your package, and these tools will roughly calculate the costs based on the weight, size, destination, and time.

Honestly, I work with more than one courier, and I have to say that working enough with a company can even get you some discounts. But you should not start your business based on this. Because that's the harsh truth - no one will offer anything for free, especially if you are the beginning of the road.

Anyway, after you find your courier or couriers, you will have to print your shipping label and attach it to your package. In case you don't know this, a shipping label is that piece of paper you have on all parcels that displays the information carriers need to deliver the package. This includes the destination address, tracking codes, and, of course, the name of the person who will need to receive the parcel. Don't start asking yourself where to get the tracking number. The courier will provide it, and both you and your customer can track it down and always see where the order is.

This being said, all you have to do is either personally go to the courier's drop-off location or schedule a pickup. Well, I personally prefer the latter but if I have to handle other chores in the city, I sometimes drop the parcels myself. Again, like in so many other aspects discussed in this book, this is also a matter of preference.

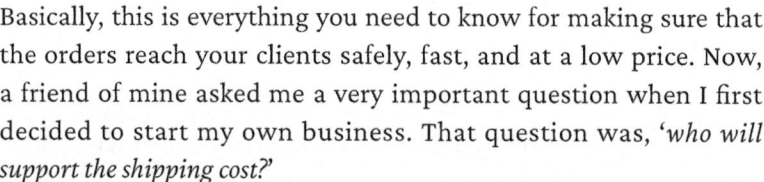

Basically, this is everything you need to know for making sure that the orders reach your clients safely, fast, and at a low price. Now, a friend of mine asked me a very important question when I first decided to start my own business. That question was, *'who will support the shipping cost?'*

As you can imagine, I didn't immediately have an answer for her. I had to think long and hard until I realized that this is actually a matter of marketing approach and I should not treat it superficially. I am in no position to tell you to offer free shipping or not. This will be for you to decide. So, I will move our discussion in that direction. But until we reach the more profound talks about marketing strategies,

I think that it's essential to understand the selling markets you can enter.

This being said, fasten your seatbelt because we are about to leave all the creative talk aside, and we will just going to talk business.

CHAPTER SEVEN

Where To Sell Your Candles

Remember how I told you about multiple market segments some chapters ago when we were at the beginning of our talks? I really hope you do, and if you don't, I will advise you to go back to chapter 3 and give it another read.

Why? Well, I will be very honest with you, and this honesty might seem a little bit too harsh. We live in a world in which it doesn't really matter how talented you are if you don't know how to sell yourself. Furthermore, we live in a world in which competition is extremely harsh.

It's true that we live in the era of the internet, which made everything easier, but it also brought together people from all around the globe. This means that you might conduct your business in New York, but you will also have competitors from Pennsylvania, Texas, as well as London or Tokyo.

I meant it when I said that sky is the limit when it comes to owning a candle-crafting company. But this also comes with some struggles and risks you will have to take.

This is why the best advice I can give you is to find your markets right from the start. The worst thing that a crafter could do is to create a marvelous product and drift without a purpose between markets, unable to find the right one.

I won't lie to you and say that you should not be intimidated by this part because it's no walk in the park, and it can literally make the difference between success and failure.

However, when you manage to find your ideal niche, you will see that finding and retaining customers is actually not that hard. Most probably, many of your future clients are already looking for you.

I know that you are probably asking yourself how you can identify the need in a market in which there are already products to satisfy anyone. The secret is always to keep your eyes open. Yes, the online world is already saturated with tons of products, leaving very little room for new business. But the good news is that the online world is also very versatile and always changing. Due to a very increased level of consumerism, people get very easily bored and look for new things to buy. And this is not necessarily because they don't like the other brands they are using. This happens because they get bored and need new stuff.

The first step you will need to take in order to identify the need is to answer a couple of questions.

The most important answer you should seek is regarding your future customers' actions. You have to figure out what they want and how much they are willing to pay for their desires.

I know that it's easier said than done, but there are ways to get inside potential clients' minds. For instance, you can see what people are already buying and try to figure out what drives them to do so. What makes them choose one brand over another? Figuring out this puzzle can launch you on the right path.

Another very good approach would be to ask yourself what you think is missing from the market and try to bring just that to the game. I mean, if you are missing it, the chances are that others feel the same way.

As scary as marketplace research might sound, I can assure you that it can be done. If I have managed to figure it out, I am sure that you will too. Furthermore, there are many tools that were created especially for this purpose.

A tool that I never thought I would use but on which I am totally dependent nowadays is Google AdWords. Many people think that this app should only be used to create ads, but that's wrong. It's actually a very good way to research keywords people are looking for. Why is this helpful? Because this could give you a better view of what they want.

For instance, let's suppose that you notice that a lot of people look for strawberry-fragranced candles, and only a few are interested in chocolate-fragranced ones. In this case, you exactly know what type of candles you should focus on.

I know that I said it before, but I will highlight it again. Always look at what competition does. It's not about stealing their ideas, but it is about getting inspired. It's about what you like about their approach and what you don't like and know that you could deliver better.

Of course, you can go directly to some brick-and-mortar shops and check out their brands, but there are other ways to research competition. What I like to do is to look at Amazon bestsellers. Why? Because it gives me a better perspective on what people are buying. Plus, it gives me direct access to their reviews.

I have to admit that when I first started my business, I also browsed some forums to see what people were talking about there, but today I only use Reddit. I don't use it to check out other discussions but sometimes go there to ask the questions I am curious about. Reddit is a very good platform to gather intel, but if you've never used it before, you might find it a little bit overwhelming and annoying.

My point here is that you should not dismiss any app or opportunity that can help you gather useful information. It doesn't matter if we are talking about social media platforms, competitors' websites, or forums. Use whatever works for you but try not to stay only in your social bubble. Go outside your group of friends and talk to other people that don't know you. It is very important to see how different people think.

Anyway, after you talk to people and realize what niche you should go to, it's time to decide where do you want to conduct your business. By this time, you should know exactly which type of candles you are going to create and, therefore, to what market target you will address.

I know that I asked you to re-read the chapter in which we talked about creating your own start-up. Even so, I want to remind you that there are three main market targets that you can focus on. I am talking about the mass market, mid-market, high-end market. Remember now? Great!

I wanted to make this recap because I am about to tell you all the ways in which you can conduct your business. However, some of them are only suited for one or two market targets. Therefore, it would be a waste of your time and money to try and sell your candles throughout those channels if you are in the wrong market target range.

But let's not fuss too much with the introductions, and let me tell you exactly what are the selling channels you can approach.

Online sales

I've talked about the importance of the internet and how lucky we are to live in such an era. You know that I hate to repeat myself when it comes to useless information. However, I do believe that some details are worth repeating, so hang with me on this one.

Long story short, online retails present many advantages. This includes low costs for launching your start-up, flexibility, and of course, good geographic reach. Another plus is that more and more people are dependent on online shopping. There are literally people who don't do physical shopping anymore. It was hard for me to believe this, but it's a fact. So many individuals are so busy and tired that they simply don't even buy their bread from the local bakery or supermarket.

The good news for you is that due to such a high demand for online shopping, a great number of tools are available to make your business shine.

Probably the most straightforward option is to create your **own website**. I know that for some of you, this might sound scary, but it actually is not such a hard task. As I said, today, we have tools that handle the hard stuff for us. In other words, you don't have to be a tech guru to design a website nowadays.

Most probably, you've heard of WordPress and how easy it is to use. Well, I have to say that I didn't find it as straightforward as others claim. And yes, I even checked out Youtube tutorials. But fear not. There are other options for people like us.

One of the most trendy platforms for starting a candle-crafting business is Shopify. The reasons for its popularity are very obvious. For once, you can very easily create any custom online store, add your social media channels, process shippings, and integrate plug-ins. Furthermore, you don't have to worry about payment methods as this tool will integrate them for you. Oh, and for everything that you don't know how to handle, Shopify has a learning tool. So, yeah, this is a wonderful app to consider.

However, recently, I discovered a new platform called Squarespace. It's not as well-known as Shopify, but it's a great choice for creative entrepreneurs that want to highlight their products using beautiful photos. And yes, you can also integrate online stores with it.

The great thing about creating your own website is that it suits all three target markets.

But if you are not very comfortable with handling your own website, you can do other types of online sales.

Many fellow candle crafters are very fond of a marketplace called **Etsy**. What is great about this platform is that it helps you reach a high number of people very fast.

Let me tell you in a few words how it works. So, you post your products for a $0.20 listing fee and 3.5% commission. I know that it may sound a lot, but as an Etsy seller, you can reach a market with more than 26 million active buyers. And I think it's worth the commission.

But since the fees are quite big, this online selling method is mostly used by crafters who wish to address mid-market and high-end target markets.

The last option for conducting online sales is through **social media channels**. In the last years, the phenomenon of social media exploded. Today, there are so many options that I don't even think I can name them all. There is Facebook, Instagram, TikTok, and I am sure that if you ask a teenager, they will tell you that all these are old news and some other platform is the new buzz these days. However, I will limit myself to what I know, but please don't reduce yourself to my obsolete tastes in social media platforms. Just take them as a starting point and research what else is out there that might suit your style.

The most obvious pick is one, or both, of the two Meta options. Both Facebook and Instagram are very popular for selling all kinds of products. You can create a business page, and you can display and sell your products from Shopify or Etsy. Furthermore, Facebook even has its own Marketplace that you can use to sell your candles locally.

The other app I think is more than suitable for this kind of business is Pinterest. What I love about it is that you can actually make direct sales through an option called "Buyable Pins." What this means is that potential customers see your candles, pin them, and they can be redirected to your Shopify store from where they can make a purchase. Pretty cool, right?

And do you know what else is cool? The fact that a social media sale is a great approach regardless of your market target. That's right. You can reach all types of potential clients with their help.

Local sales

I know that we live in an era in which online marketing is considered to be a must. But just as some people only do online shopping, there are also others who wish to keep things more or less traditional. And these individuals like to go to local events and talk to the crafters. The good news? Having the possibility to create a personal rapport with clients is actually a tremendous plus for you, and I will tell you exactly why that is.

Getting in real contact with your potential clients gives them the opportunity to touch and smell your candles. In other words, they can see for themselves that you are a serious crafter, selling high-quality products.

So, where do you think these one-on-one sale opportunities might be? There are two main events that you can target: farmers' markets and fairs or festivals.

Let's take each at a time and understand their implications.

I don't know about you, but I absolutely love all types of farmers' markets. I love to find genuine products and goods. And after I became a crafter, I learned to appreciate them even more.

Anyway, if you are interested in selling locally, you should see what kind of markets are around you. There is a website of the National Farmers Market Directory that will give you more details about what's going on in your proximity.

However, you should keep in mind that at local markets you won't be able to sell super expensive products. This means that this way of conducting business applies if you are targeting mass markets and maybe lower-mid ones.

Another option you have to make physical sales is at fairs and festivals. Basically, the approach is very similar to the previous one, so I won't linger too much on the matter.

However, I will tell you that you can very easily find these events on social media platforms such as Facebook. Also, you can check out other websites like Crafter Lister or Festival Net. And I know that this might sound deprecated, but you can even visit your local chamber of commerce's website. You might be surprised to find very nice events posted there.

Wholesaling

Finally, you could focus on an approach called wholesaling. Don't worry if you've never heard of this term before because it only sounds fancy.

Wholesaling is just a word that sums up selling merchandise in bulk to various retailers for reselling purposes. Simply put, you sell large quantities of your candles at once and are not in direct contact with the final client.

What you need to know right now is that wholesaling can be done using various channels.

First of all, there are the local shops that you can consider contacting. This is the easiest way to step into the world of wholesaling. The nice thing about local shops is that you can actually get to know the owners, you can talk to them and share opinions at any time.

Of course, once you get ahold of how this approach works, you should not limit yourself to just the local shops but also target other states.

Anyway, I love the idea of working with shops, especially boutiques, as it gives me a sense of a professional and luxurious world.

However, you should keep in mind that this wholesaling world is mostly suitable for mid and high-end market targets.

Finally, remember how I told you about Etsy? The amazing fact about this platform is that not only you can use it for online sales, but it can also give you access to their Etsy Wholesale. And that means more than 25k stores.

Of course, this can't be done overnight. You need to be a consistent Etsy seller, have a professional attitude, and have competitive prices. Yet, this is indeed a milestone you should want to achieve.

Well, this is everything you need to know about selling markets to start your business. Of course, you can, and you should not stick just to one selling market. You can combine online sales with local sales or wholesaling. You should definitely do it. But not right from the start. In the beginning, focus on just one approach and do it well. After you master that funnel, go ahead and conquer the next. It's only natural to do so.

Anyhow, I know I said it before, but I will tell you again. Yes, figuring out what selling market to choose sounds like an impossible task, but it's not. You just have to learn how to listen. That's all. There's literally no rocket science around this. It's all about patience and listening. It's about letting go of your misconceptions and understanding how the world actually is.

So with these thoughts in mind, I want to move along and tackle one last complicated topic. That's it. You are down to one. After that, there will be only some more answers, and you are all set. But until you cross that beautiful finish line, you have one more task - deciding on a marketing approach.

CHAPTER EIGHT

Marketing Strategy

As we are reaching the end of our journey, I want to be as honest as possible with you. Not that I haven't been throughout the book. No. I have always told you the truth, even though sometimes I might have sounded harsh.

Anyway, let me give you the awful facts. Creating successful marketing strategies and campaigns requires skills that not many possess. Truth be told, there even are some marketing companies that only apply patterns without understanding the product or the brand.

So, if you can afford it, I strongly recommend you talk with a marketing specialist. It will make total sense to do it, especially if you have absolutely no background in the domain.

Regardless of what you will decide, I will create a draft of what your approach should look like, but keep in mind that what you'll read here is pure theory, and I can't actually craft both a strategy and a campaign for you. For once, I don't even know your business model, mission, or vision.

What I will do in this chapter is to explain the steps any marketing approach should take. Using them, you can then create a plan by yourself or with a marketing specialist. Is everything clear? Great! Let's begin!

You probably know this, but here it is nevertheless. When a business just starts to show its face in this big and crowded market, most business owners just go with the flow and try to keep their current customers happy. They even go that extra mile just to make sure that they receive a referral or testimonial.

Anyway, some years back, I took a marketing class. Back then, and yes, there are more years in the middle than I like to confess, our lecturer told us that we live in a world in which new clients find new companies. He implied that this happens without too much initial effort from the business owner. Well, those were the days, my friend. And what lovely days they were.

Unfortunately for you, me, and all the other people struggling to make it out there, those days are well gone, and today, you really have to make an effort to stand out from the crowd.

The reality is that to attract new customers and to do it on a predictable basis. You will have to make lots of marketing efforts. Now, the reason why I said predictable is that you don't want to find yourself in a mambo-jumbo random situation in which sometimes, an individual visits your website, and if you are really lucky, she places an order. No. You want to be able to predict how sales will go and make plans accordingly.

So before anything else, let me explain in simple words what is a marketing campaign because I really think that many people use this term without actually understanding its meaning.

If you strip the notion of a marketing campaign of all its fancy academic words, you will be left with an initiative that has the desired outcome, a budget, plus a start and end date. I will go even further and set an example so that you understand 100% what I am trying to say.

So, you've just opened your candle business and wish to attract new clients from a specific area. Let's say, Brooklyn, just for the sake of it. You prepare your event on social media, plan a budget and decide that for a week, women between 20 and 45 from Brooklyn will receive your advertisement on Facebook. This example here is what exactly a marketing campaign looks like.

Now, one of the biggest mistakes many people make is to assume that a project that has no start and end date is a campaign. Please don't go there. If you are doing a task over and over again without stopping it, then it is called a marketing strategy and not a campaign. Basically, it's part of what your brand represents as a business. I hope that it's all clear.

I will split this chapter into two main categories. This way, I hope that you will not miss anything important on the matter and will at least have a broad idea of how to start your marketing approaches.

Marketing Strategy

I know that I succinctly introduced you to this term, but I feel the need to explain it a little more. So, a marketing strategy is what describes your whole business plan from finding leads, turning these leads into customers, and in the end, retaining them.

From a theoretical perspective, a marketing strategy has a value proposition, a key brand messaging, and data on target customers.

Now, I could tell you about the 4P's of marketing, but this is not what you are here for. You are here to understand some key takeaways and apply them to your business.

As I previously mentioned, a marketing strategy should not have a start and an end date. But that doesn't mean that if you see that the plan is not working, you should not change it.

The reason why I described it as a long-lasting lifespan is that this strategy contains, or at least should contain, all the key elements that make your brand unique, elements that should hold for as long as possible.

I am no marketing specialist, but in my humble opinion, I believe that the most important goal of any marketing strategy is to be able to communicate your brand's competitive advantages. Simply put, you should be able to let people know why your business is better than the next one.

This is why I was telling you that knowing your market and doing very detailed analysis and research is such important for your success. Knowing your competition is a very powerful weapon.

I am sure that by now, many of you are '*okay, great talk, but what does a marketing strategy look like?*'

Well, imagine a big bowl in which you add every attempt you make to increase sales: PR campaigns, initiatives, advertising, and outreach but also market research, pricing decision, tailored messages for specific demographics, service promotion, and so on.

Now, it's impossible for me to divide and conquer all these aspects in such a way that you understand them without writing another book just for marketing purposes.

So if you don't want to hire a specialist to guide you throughout the process of drafting your marketing strategy, I can only suggest that you use tools and templates that are available online.

One of the best, in my opinion, is Hubspot. There is a very detailed article on every step you have to take in order to build a solid approach. However, feel free to check on other platforms and see what speaks more to you.

Marketing Campaign

Now that you know the basic difference between the two terms, it's a little bit easier for me to extend the discussion.

The good news about the campaign is that you do A/B testing and see what works and what doesn't. Of course, that involves money and time, and I am pretty sure that you can't afford to lose any.

So the best thing to do at this point is to try and follow some templates. It doesn't matter which one you'll choose, as they are many all over the internet. What matters is that you include some very important parts which I will immediately tell you about. However, just for the sake of argument, I have to advise you once again to see what Hubspot has to offer.

Anyhow, one of the most important things to establish is your immediate goal. You will have to identify this goal for each campaign you'll run. To measure each success, you will need to use some metrics such as newsletter subscriptions, sales, clicks, and so on. These metrics are different from one campaign to the next.

The only advice I can think to give you here is to try and set your goal as quantifiable as possible. Why? Because it is easier to keep track of it using the metrics I was telling you about, and it also can give you a clear view of the results.

Let me give you a clear example of some of the metrics you can use. For instance, you can start by collecting the email addresses of your leads. One goal would be to have at least 100 newsletter subscribers in a month. And speaking of leads, another goal would be to transform at least 10% of your leads into buying customers within a given time.

That's how specific you should be. Anyway, regardless of the metrics you use, the goals should be more or less the same for everyone. So let me tell you the most frequent ones: increase sales, get new customers, promote new products, improve retention rate, and raise brand awareness.

In other words, these are the targets you should be aiming for.

The next step is to decide on the channel you will going to use. You have to plan your campaign based on where you will going to run it. It would be a total waste to apply the same tactics on Facebook and Twitter. Yes, they are both social media platforms, but they work extremely differently. So, the first thing you should do is to understand the channel and tailor your campaign based on it.

And if you are wondering if the content should also be different based on these channels, the answer is yes. You will have to identify what works and distribute it throughout the campaign.

But let's stay a little bit more on this topic. Marketing campaigns can be extremely simple, but they can also be twisted and complex. And one of the main ingredients of this complexity is given by the channels you use to promote yourself.

I mentioned two of the most popular social media platforms just a few seconds ago. But social media is not the only channel that you can and should use. The most regularly used channels are social media, of course, but also email, direct mail, radio, TV, print, and digital media, advertising, and events.

However, when you are at the beginning of the road, some of these channels make no sense. For instance, TV advertising. I know that we haven't talked about the budget yet, but let's face it. You most probably won't afford to sponsor a post on TV. So, you should focus on more appropriate channels. Of course, you will decide on your own what suits you and what doesn't, but most often than not, new companies focus on social media, trade shows, email, and events. But again, do your research before you invest in such a channel. You might discover that a billboard is what drives your clients to you.

A word of advice - remember what is your target market and go to the channels they are most likely to use. A thing that I learned is that millennials love social media, but Baby Boomers are not as fond. On the other hand, millennials hate to receive emails when the other category doesn't have a problem even receiving direct promotional mail.

Another very important aspect is the way you design your campaign. Yes, you read that right. People want to be attracted to your campaign. Otherwise, they won't click to find out more about what you have to say. Therefore, you will have to identify the elements that attract your target group and use them wisely.

Designing your marketing campaign has the sole purpose of making your leads do whatever you wish them to. I know that this sounds bad, but that's the way it is. In marketing terms, it's called 'call-to-action (CTA).' Of course, you can create campaigns with multiple CTA, but I suggest you keep it simple. Asking people to do more than one thing will disorientate your leads and will make them back down. So, just one CTA per campaign is more than enough.

But let's return to the design part. If the word *design* sounds scary, you should not feel intimidated by it. Yes, a few years back, businesses had to rely on advertising agencies to design their campaign content. However, today the internet is full of helpful apps such as Canva, Gimp, or iMovie that will help you create beautiful and interactive content.

Finally, there is the matter of budget. Unfortunately, just like in most cases, you can't do much without the right capital. And, of course, no social media platform will promote your content if you don't pay the right price. I mean, why would they when your competition is willing to pay better?

But don't get scared. The only thing I want to highlight is that you should keep track of your budget and find ways to produce powerful marketing campaigns based on how much you afford to pay. The last thing you want is to end up with an amazing project that has no way to be funded.

But how much can you afford? I mean, is there a way to know how much you could spend on advertising? Well, yes, and again I want to highlight the benefits of talking to a marketing specialist. But again, you can do some calculations on your own as well. One of the easiest easy is to calculate the customer lifetime value (CLTV).

This is a very easy mathematical formula that sounds like this:

CLTV = (Average Value of a Sale) X (Number of Repeat Transactions) X (Average Retention Time in Months or Years for a Typical Customer)

Having this data will help you get at least an estimation of how many clients a campaign can bring it. This is realistically speaking and not what social media claims when you prepare an ad.

Anyway, after you launch each campaign, you will have to monitor it. You will need to keep track of the results and see if they are getting close to your goal or not. After the campaign reaches its end, you will have to determine if the results were satisfactory or not. Having really clear expectations makes it very easy to understand if the struggles paid off or not. Furthermore, after each such event, you should take the time and understand if the campaign was actually helpful and if you should repeat it or not. You should also understand why it caused you to get frustrated and if you could have done things differently. But the most important part is to see if this approach you are taking is correct or if you are operating under very wrong assumptions.

Some Marketing Tips

I know that up until now, I have only talked about generic marketing solutions and didn't necessarily give you the information you were looking for. As I said, I can't create a marketing strategy or campaign for you, but here are some tips that are known to work for our business.

I will suppose that you already have a killer logo and brand, so I won't tell you again how important this part is. Also, I won't repeat myself to say how vital it is to create beautiful and personalized packaging. Visual sells, and that is one of the most valuable marketing tips I can offer.

Another thing that I can tell you is to make sure that your social media accounts are always active and linked to your website.

Don't think that if you managed to create a nice brand, it's enough to survive in this world. Invest and reinvest in its identity. Create brand awareness by all means. Distribute business cards wherever you can. Did you know that Pinterest's owner went to each Apple store he could find and opened his website on all phones, tablets, and computers he could put his hands on? Why? Because the next people that came after him to see the app.

What I am trying to say is that there is no shame in promoting your business in any way you can.

A great way to create brand awareness is to participate in community events. This way, you will get in direct touch with sociable people, and you will be able to build trust. It doesn't matter if the event is not necessarily candle-related. Most probably, the hosts will want to create an atmosphere, and, of course, candles are a great way to do so. Contact the organizers and offer your products for free or at a great discount that they can't refuse. This is a great way to make people hear about you. Yes, you might not gain immediate profit, but it's worth a try.

And since we are at the free stuff talk, you should know that people are crazy about giveaways. This can open many doors for marketing campaigns and strategies. You can give away some of your candles, or you can get into partnerships with other brands. For instance, contact a library and set up a giveaway together. This way, you can reach multiple leads by combining your customers' pools.

Now, what I am about to tell you next is an approach loved by some and hated by others. I am talking about referral programs. This is a great exclusive path to use your clients to work for your benefit. Again, not the best choice of words, but it is what it is. Brand ambassadors are a great way to reach people that you have no other way of reaching and give back to discounts and new opportunities for your clients.

Now, many people will tell you that newsletters are great for keeping your customers informed. I won't deny it. These emails have the power to spread your words easily and in a convincing manner. Furthermore, they work as reminders, and with the right title and content, they can even score you some sales. The only problem is that people hate spam. And these days, not many individuals care for their advertising emails. Send them on the wrong day and hour, and you will end up with a big list of unsubscriptions. However, yes, email marketing is a good approach, but only if it's done properly.

If you are good with words, you can even start writing blog articles if you are good with words. This can help you get more personal with your clients and can help you with your SEO struggles. And now, you are probably asking - but in the world is SEO? SEO means Search Engine Optimization, and it represents the process that helps you gain free traffic from the search engines, such as Google. Simply put, the better your SEO score, the higher your position in the search result pages, and therefore, the more people will see it.

Naturally, if you decide to go with a blog, you can write whatever you want there. However, I suggest that you keep it as close to the candle topic as possible. For instance, you can write about safety measures, decoration ideas, the difference between waxes, and so on.

After you gain some notoriety, you can even record videos and share tutorials on Youtube.

Basically, what I am trying to say is that you can do whatever you want and see if it works in your favor. Try to be as creative as possible not only when crafting your candles but also when conceiving marketing strategies and campaigns. Because in the end, this, too, is somehow a piece of art.

CHAPTER NINE

Troubleshooting

A nd that's a wrap, my friends! This is everything there is to know about the candle-making business. I know it was a long journey, but I do hope that it was also a fun one. I won't keep you busy for very long. I just want to tell you that I tried to answer some of the most frequently asked questions regarding our topic. The reason why I decided to add this extra chapter is that I know that many people still have questions even after reading a theoretical book. So, I do hope that this can make even more light and help you put together the last puzzle pieces.

Q: How to clean a votive container?

A: There is more than one way to do this, but I will tell you about the safest way. Heat up your oven at the lowest possible setting. Place the votive container on a baking sheet and let it heat in the oven for about 10 minutes. Using oven mitts, take it out of the oven and rub

Q: What is tunneling?

A: Tunneling is an outcome that occurs when only a very small amount of wax melts around the wick. So, instead of melting the wax on all the surfaces of the candle, the flame is consuming only the immediate wax, creating a small and vertical tunnel.

Q: Is it worth it to start my own candle-making business?

A: If you are serious and passionate about this domain, then the answer is definitely yes. But as you already know it will be easy. Yet, once you bypass the obstacles, you are in for a fun and relaxing job.

Q: How good should I be before starting my own candle-making business?

A: Well, there is no measuring when it comes to talent. However, I think that if you would consider spending money on a candle similar to what you are crafting, then you should also think that others would do too. This is the moment when you can really think about starting a business.

Q: Are scented candles really safe?

A: I know that we've been over this part, but I want to highlight it once more. Well-made candles are safe regardless if they are odorless or scented. They become dangerous only if they don't burn clean and release toxic chemicals.

Q: Are petroleum-based candles safe?

A: There is no scientific evidence that specifies that burning paraffin wax candles can cause any harm to your health.

Q: Can a scented candle trigger my asthma or allergies?

A: As I previously said, scented candles are known to be very safe if done right. However, there are some peoples who are allergic to a specific component. So, individuals who know to be sensitive to some fruits or herbs should not burn candles that have them in their composition.

Q: Should I be concerned about wicks that contain lead?

A: Wicks with lead are dangerous. However, they've been officially banned. Well, at least in the US. However, you should be careful if you order wicks that are imported from countries that don't respect this norm.

Q: Is the soot harmful?

A: Long story short, no, the soot produced by candles is not harmful to the environment. It is just an itsy bitsy tiny byproduct of incomplete combustion.

Q: Is it true that scented candles can produce more soot than odorless ones?

A: Soot is a result of an improper burning process which is directly linked to the wick and the flame. However, certain fragrances can increase the amount of soot, but only slightly.

Q: How long can the fragrance of a candle last?

A: Well, technically, a candle should not lose its scent for at least one year if it's not burned. But of course, there are many aspects that influence this fact.

Q: How many times can I use a scented candle?

A: There is no exact science here. However, if you don't burn your candles too often, you will help them retain their fragrance for an extended period of time. So, my advice is to light it only once every 24 hours.

Q: Should you keep a window open when burning candles?

A: Most definitely not. As a matter of fact, you should avoid any proximity to air conditioners, fans, or opened windows. Moving air disturbs the flame, creating soot and black marks.

Q: Is there something that I should definitely avoid when crafting my candles?

A: Avoid using cheap and unsafe raw materials. It doesn't matter how talented you are if the products you are using can cause your clients problems.

Q: Where does the wax go when burning candles?

A: Most of the candle's matter that results from burning evaporated in the air in the form of water vapors and carbon dioxide.

Q: Can candles expire?

A: Yes, but not in the same sense as food products. Of course, in time, they can certainly suffer degradation processes. What can happen is that if you leave them for years, standing on a shelve is not to burn properly or to have a hard time lighting them.

Q: Why do candles' flames always point up?

A: It's due to physics, actually. The flame heats up the surrounding air, creating currents around itself. Thanks to the heat, the air is thinner, making sure that the flame rises.

Q: How long does it take to make a proper first burn?

A: When you light up a candle for the first time, you should let it burn for one hour per inch of container diameter.

Q: Can I support myself by only selling candles?

A: This is really up to you and how serious you plan to be. But if you are willing to give all it takes, then yes. As we've already talked about in this book, the candle industry is a pretty profitable business. Therefore, you can no debatably make a living out of selling candles.

Q: Are some fragrances more popular than others?

A: People are unique, and naturally, so are their preferences. However, I noticed that some odors are more popular than others among my clients.

This being said, my customers generally love citrus, vanilla, red currant, and patchouli. But again, you need to see what works for your clients and go from there.

Q: Do clients look for something specific when choosing their candles?

A: Again, this is a matter of preference, but I will tell you how I choose the products I use, regardless if we talk about candles or other stuff. When I don't know a brand, I always look at things such as presentation, ingredients, and other little things such as smell.

Q: Is there such thing as a relaxing fragrance?

A: I love the smell of vanilla because it reminds me of my childhood. However, not everybody shares my enthusiasm. This is why I can tell you that, as a general rule, lavender is a very relaxing fragrance, which is good for calming down and falling asleep.

Q: Is it true that candles can cure depression?

A: Just like aromatherapy, lighting candles can help you ease stress and relax your mind and body. Even so, I won't go claiming that candles can cure depression. But they can improve the total psychological well-being, therefore, can reduce anxiety and fear.

Q: Are there any candles really popular?

A: A lot of people want to copy what already is known to work. Unfortunately, there is no perfect recipe that will help you drive sales and make you popular. This is why I suggest you really study the market before you create your prototypes.

Beeswax candles are super loved by many but rejected by others due to the fact that they are not vegan. Soy wax candles are popular among vegans but are not very cherished by others.

Once you realize that you cannot please everybody, you should be just fine.

Q: Is there such things as the perfect candle size?

A: I would say that it depends on the type of candle. However, it is my firm belief that you should use candles based on the size of the room you light them on is. For example, for a medium-sized living room, go with a 7-10 oz candle, while for your bathroom, choose a smaller one of 2-6 oz.

Q: Is there a timeframe I should consider before lighting up a candle?

A: There is no exact science here. However, I do recommend you let your candles set. I would suggest waiting for somewhere between 24 to 48 hours when it comes to paraffin candles and for 5-7 days for soy and beeswax ones.

Q: Is there a way to easily recognize a good quality candle?

A: There are many small details to check before you can state if a candle is high-quality or not. For instance, you can look at the size of the flame. You want it to be big enough and stand mighty and tall. Furthermore, you don't want your candle to produce soot or dripping.

Q: Do I need to let my candles cure?

A: The short answer is yes. But let me tell you exactly why that is. Naturally, you can burn your candle even if it's not cured. Moreover, it will physically burn perfectly fine. However, if it is a fragranced candle, the odor will be blunt and not as strong as if it would if you had waited.

Q: Is it true that I should not burn a candle for more than 4 hours?

A: Basically, this is a true fact. If you do let your candle burn for more than 4 hours at a time, the wick will collect carbon, increasing the risk of mushrooming. Just to remind you, this means an unstable flame, smoke, and soot. In other words, everything you don't want in a candle.

Q: Do I really have to wait for a week before I burn one of my just-made soy candles?

A: As I've mentioned before, soy candles need curing time. Letting them rest for 5-7 days will allow the fragrance to really bind with the soy wax and give the best results.

Q: Is there a recommended timeframe for drying candle wax?

A: We've spoken about this part during the manufacturing chapter. But just as a reminder, you should let the wax dry for as much as possible before you take it out of the mold. If you rush the process, you will only end up with cracks. Of course, if this happens, you can reheat the wax and repeat the process. But is it worth it? I guess not. So, wait and give the wax time to set.

Q: I want to make 10 oz candles. How much fragrance should I put in there?

A: The best thing I can suggest is to follow the manufacturer's instructions. Each brand is different, and you should really trust the people behind it. However, as a general rule, you should consider around 1 oz per pound of wax.

Q: Can I sleep with a lit candle around?

A: The first rule of burning candles is to never let them be unsupervised. All right? Why? For the obvious reasons, of course. The candle's container will get hotter and hotter while it burns, and this can really increase the risk of danger.

Furthermore, you already know that you should not burn candles for more than 4 hours at a time.

Q: Is it true that candles can cause mucus?

A: This really depends on how sensitive a person is. Basically, being around a burning candle is very similar to being around a person who is smoking.

In other words, if you are sensitive, a scented candle will trigger the same symptoms as cigarette smoke. These symptoms include watery eyes, runny nose, and headaches.

Q: Can I place my candles in the freezer?

A: Remember how I told you about placing the molds in the freezer for a couple of minutes to manage to take out the candles with ease? Well, at the same time, I advised you not to leave them there for too long because frozen candles can crack.

So, yes, you can place the candle in the freezer before burning it, reducing the melt time. But make sure that you don't let it sit there for too long.

Q: Can candles produce carbon monoxide?

A: Yes, burning candles produce carbon monoxide just like any other burning element. Although the risk of them causing carbon monoxide poisoning is not very high, you should still be careful about this.

Q: Is it true that salt helps candles burn for longer periods of time?

A: Simply put, salt does more or less the same thing as placing the candles in the freezer - it slows down the melting rate. What does that mean? It means that you will get a longer economic burn.

Q: Can I use a candle to warm up a room?

A: Burning candles indeed produce some heat. But let's be logical about it. A candle is small, and therefore its heat is not strong enough to heat an entire room.

Q: Can I use glitter when making my candles?

A: No. Never. And I mean it. Don't you ever use glitter when crafting your candles! It can really damage the burning process and produce accidents.

Q: Can I put gold flakes in my candles.

A: Yes. Gold foil is safe to be used. Furthermore, they offer great designs if used properly. What I want to state is that using gold foil right, you can create candles that are truly beautiful pieces of decoration.

Q: Can I cause a fire by lighting candles?

A: Yes, if you are not careful, you can cause a fire by lighting candles. As a matter of fact, it is known that candles caused more than 15k fires in residential areas that led to more than 100 deaths and 1000 injuries. Most recently than not, the reasons for these fires were the candle's very close proximity to combustible material.

Q: So, what are the places to avoid placing a burning candle?

A: As a general rule, you should avoid any places with a draft, in reach of children or pets, and those that are too close to any flammable material. This includes any curtains, towels, and so on.

Q: Are there any cheaper imitation gold leaves I could use for my candles?

A: There are some golden leaves made out of a material called Dutch metal. It is true that they are cheaper, but it also tarnishes over time.

Q: After I blow my candle, should I put the lid on it?

A: If your candle has a lid, then yes. Covering your candle with a lid will help you keep it safe from dust and dirt, will trap any potential smoke, and will also also keep the fragrance in for longer periods of time.

Q: Can I provoke a sinus infection by burning candles?

A: I know that this kind of question keeps popping up, but many people are traumatized by the possibility of getting sick. This is why I want to eliminate all doubts on the matter.

So, just as previously mentioned, this is not a yes or no kind of question. It really depends on how sensitive a person is. Because, yes, sinus infections can be provoked by pollutants such as synthetic smells. On the other hand, most often than not, this doesn't happen, and sinus infections are simply caused by viruses, and the fact that you were around a burning candle is simply a coincidence.

Q: Is placing the candle in the fridge the same as placing it in the freezer?

A: Let's see what you know so far. You know that keeping your candles for a short period of time in the freezer is a benefic thing, but keep it too long, and you will end up having cracked candles. The same applies to the fridge. Of course, the cooling process takes longer, but the outcomes are more or less the same.

Q: Should I always use a candle lid?

A: First of all, not all candles are suitable for having lids. However, the ones they do, such as candle jars, should be used accordingly. This means that you should keep the lid and use it every time you extinguish the flame.

Q: Is there a special way to store candles after crafting them?

A: Each crafter has its own technique. Therefore, I can only tell you about what I tend to do. So, I wrap them in paper tissue and store them in a cool place. This way, I make sure I don't lose fragrance, and there is no risk of the candles melting.

Q: Is there a hack to prevent the melting of my candles while in storage?

A: As previously said, wrap them in paper or bubble wrap, then place them on a flat row. If needed, when working with tapers, you can stack the rows on top of each other. However, be careful not to put heavier models on them.

Q: Is there a right temperature for storing candles?

A: I try to keep my temperature constant at around 68 °F (20 °C). However, you can store your products at any temperature between 50 °F (10 °C) and 85 °F (29 °C).

Q: Should I store some of my candles upside down?

A: Basically, no. Especially if we are talking about pillar and jar candles. Some claim that if you store candles upside down, you prevent the wick from getting stuck in the wax. But if a candle is a crafter properly, you won't have this kind of problem.

Q: Which one is better? Soy or beeswax candles?

A: Again, I know that we have already talked about this aspect, but since it is such a controversial one, I feel the need to approach it one last time.

First of all, one is vegan, and the other one is not. So depending on your beliefs and lifestyle, one will win in this category. One needs some chemical process to reach its final state. The other one doesn't. Again, a matter of preference.

Finally, there is a matter of burning. Soy wax burns with a cool white flame is odorless unless you use a fragrance. On the other hand, beeswax burns with a more natural light and has a sweet and lovely natural odor. This being said, each person has their own favorite wax type when it comes to candles.

Q: Is there such thing as a healthy candle wax?

A: Remember the story of my grandmother and her approach to lighting candles for keeping fungi away? So, yeah, beeswax candles are indeed the healthiest choice out there. The scientific part behind this statement is actually easy to understand. When they burn properly, beeswax candles release negative ions that ensure clean air. In other words, they work as air purifiers.

Q: Why is my wax melt produces smoke?

A: Sometimes, melting wax can release a vapor that looks like a white smoke. This being said, this is only the oil evaporating, and it is totally normal. Therefore, there is nothing to be concern about.

Chapter Ten

Glossary

Since there might be a few terms that I used, and you didn't recognize, I decided to help you with a glossary. These are some of the most popular terms that will pop up during the candle-making process. They are in alphabetical order, so feel free to browse them any way you want. Let's go.

A

Additive

This substance is blended with wax to enhance the burning features or alter its effects. Additives may contain stearic acid or different types of UV inhibitors.

Afterglow

Afterglow is the light coming after removing any energy source. Even after extinguishing, a wick may continue to "glow" and burn slightly more.

B

Beads (wax)

Beads represent that type of wax processed into tiny beads for making the candle-making process easier. The smaller the beads, the faster they will melt.

Beeswax

As the name suggests, beeswax is created by bees and then processed to remove all the impurities from the comb. The quality of this wax and its characteristics depends on the colony's diet, location, health, number of members, and location from where the wax has been gathered.

Beeswax usually has a higher melting point than other types of waxes and needs larger wicks, capable of delivering sufficient heat to provide fuel. Beeswax is ideal for tapers rather than containers because of its capacity to reach the appropriate temperature.

Burn rate

Burn rate defines the amount of wax that melts during an hour or the time needed for the wax in a candle to burn completely.

Burn Cycle

The action of burning a candle for 4 hours and then blowing it to let the wax cool. This process helps evaluate wick performance and calculate the burning time cycle.

C

Candle

A firing unit that stabilizes heat with fuel and oxygen to provide a relaxing effect. Some candles have pleasant fragrances, making them a natural perfume diffuser.

Chatter Marks

Chatter marks can be horizontal lines or rings that appear once the wax is poured into a cold mold or container, or once the wax is poured at too cool of a temperature.

Coconut Wax

Coconut wax is derived from coconut oil, and it is extracted through different methods right from the core of a coconut. The processes include hydrogenation and periodic combination with other types of waxes. This way, the coconut wax melting point increases and keeps the solid shape at ambient temperature.

Cold Throw

Cold throw represents the perfume delivered from a candle without burning.

Container Candle

Any type of candle that is poured right into the container from which it will light up and burn.

Core

The core represents the "heart" of a candle. The term is used to describe the inner material of a candle wick (for instance, cotton, zinc, or paper).

Coreless

It refers to no core material wicks.

Cure

A candle needs to cure the wax to set or age and help the fragrance keep its bold or subtle scent.

D

Diameter

Diameter is a measurement for candles, containers, or molds at their widest point.

Double boiler

Two nested pans on top of each other, with water in the lower one, are placed to allow moderate heating.

Double Scenting

Adding one ounce of perfume per pound of wax.

Dye

Specific types of colorants for wax.

E

Essential oil

A type of oil derived from a natural substance (flowers, leaves, plant material, grass, wood).

F

Flakes

Flakes (wax flakes) are made from wax transformed into fragile flakes for effortless candle production. The smaller the fragments, the easier they will melt due to reducing mass.

Flashpoint

Flashpoint is the temperature at which a specific substance can catch fire if it comes in contact with a spark or an open flame.

Floater

This refers to a floating candle that has a main tapered base that flows once placed in water.

Fragrance Oil

Unlike essential oils, which come with one hundred percent natural sources, fragrance oils blend synthetic and genuine parts to create scented oils.

Frosting

A bright dusty substance that pops out in soy wax candles. Icing does not influence the burning process, and it is not harmful at all. Frosting will not diminish the scent of candles.

Fragrance Load

Fragrance load represents a load of perfume added by weight used as a base percentage. For instance, one oz. of perfume put into 1 lb of wax represents a 6 percent load.

G

Gel Candle

A gel candle is a transparent material derived from a mineral oil-based product.

Glass Adhesion

Glass adhesion is popular as Delamination or Wet Spots. This happens when the wax detaches from the glass. Glass adhesion often happens with container candles.

Gutter

Gutter stands for the excess of melted wax pulling out of a self-standing candle.

H

Hang-Up

Hang-up is the unburned wax that remains on the jar's walls when the candle has entirely burned.

Hot Throw

The perfume comes from a burning candle.

Hurricane Candle

Hurricane candle describes the external part of wax that has a high with a high liquefying point. This type of candle can be decorated and used as simple ornamentation. Candlemakers will add an inner candle in the middle of hurricane wax to be burned or replaced.

J

Jump lines

The unplanned lines appear on the sides of a pillar candle or a container. These lines are often a cause of wax pouring at a too low temperature or pouring it into a cold container. The wax will immediately harden and start to set as long as more wax is poured right on top of the cured one.

M

Melt point

Melt point is the temperature at which wax starts becoming liquid.

Melt Pool

The soft wax as candles burns.

Mix Temperature

The ideal temperature to add fragrance and color to the melted wax is around 185 degrees Fahrenheit, regardless of the type of wax used.

Mold

A specific shape is used to create an unfree candle. These forms are usually made of metal.

Mold plug

Conically formed rubber items are meant to close the hole in the foundation of a mold.

Mold Release

A particular medium is used to cover the inside of a mold to ease removing the candle.

Mold Sealer

A substance with the consistency of clay is used to secure the hole on the bottom of the mold. Mold sealer covers all the extra space that appears around the wick on the external side of the mold.

Mottling

An effect on the wax surface that looks like a snowflake.

Material Safety Data Sheet (MSDS)

A manual of safety information put together by candle manufacturers and marketers.

Mushrooming

Carbon growth on the top of the wick appears after burning.

N

Neck

The vertical ray of the wich, securing the tab of the wick. The stretch of the wick strip can vary.

O

Opaque

A surface that is not reflecting or sharing light; impenetrable to sight.

Overdip

The action of coating a candle with a different wax for decor or color purposes.

Out of Bottle

The first analysis of a fragrance as soon as someone opens the candle bottle. This applies to as out of bottle or OOB consideration.

P

Palm Wax

As the name suggests, palm wax is a gummy wax made from palm. This medium burns cleanly and is an excellent alternative to paraffin.

Paraffin Wax

Paraffin wax is made of refined petroleum, and it is one of the most popular materials in candle making.

Parasoy Wax

Parasoy is a blend of soy and paraffin wax. This mixture has been done to take advantage of the good characteristics of both resins and obtain a good-quality candle.

Pillar Candle

Pillar candle is made in a mold and built to be a free-standing product.

Pour Temperature

The ideal temperature to pour color or fragrance into the mold or container.

Power Burn

The process of burning a candle is longer than 4 hours, often going up to 8+ hours. This act can be dangerous, and it is not recommended without supervision.

MELISSA FARRELL

Primed

Primed is a term that refers to wicking; it means the act of coating with wax.

R

Relief holes

Holes inserted in candles to let out air pockets that can appear as soon as the wax cools. This step is recommended before pouring the second layer of wax.

Repour

The process of stuffing the hole left once the wax cured and level the candle until its top.

S

Scent Load

The amount of fragrance a candle wax can support; the quantity is usually stated in a percentage.

Scent oil

This is the equivalent of fragrance oil.

Scent Throw

The perfume released by a candle.

Second Pour

The same meaning as the "Repour".

Single Pour Wax

A specific wax that won't shrink. No need to pour a second layer.

Sinkhole

A sinkhole represents the hole formed when the wax cures and hardens.

Smelly Jelly

This is a product formed of water crystals, added as an air freshener, without being heated.

Soy Wax

A type of wax that is one hundred percent natural.

Stearic Acid

Stearic acid is a substance used to improve the opaqueness of wax, making it slow burn and harden quicker.

Stuttering

Shuttering means the same with chatter marks.

Synthetic Oil

Fragrance oil made artificially.

T

Taper

A thin and tall candle that becomes slimmer at the burning end. People must use a candle holder for this type of taper candle.

Tart

A tart candle is a small amount of perfumed wax for a tart burner. Tart can be made in different shapes, but usually, it has a 2.5" diameter.

Tart Burner

A special device, similar to a tealight, with a lower compartment for a tea candle and an open cupped area on top for heating the tart.

Tealight

A tiny, self-contained candle, mostly poured in a tin cup, with 1.5"diameter and 0.5" height.

Transition Temperature

The temperature range at which a wax transforms from a liquid to a solid state.

Triple Scent

The act of pouring a specific amount of fragrance per pound of wax.

Tunneling

The tunneling effect appears when the wick does not make a complete melt pool in a candle and leaves a specific ring of unmelted wax on the exterior sides.

U

UV Stabilizer

A preservative to prevent the candle from fading when revealed to UV rays and fluorescent lighting.

V

Viscosity

Viscosity measures the fluid's fight to flow. While honey or ketchup has a high viscosity, juice and milk have a low thickness.

Votive Candle

A small type of candle, with a diameter of 1.75" and a height of 2". This type requires a votive holder when it burns; it is also designed to ultimately come in a fluid shape.

Vybar

A type of polymer that is used to make the fragrance long-lasting. Vybar increases the wax opacity and intensifies the color. This product is the latest substitute for stearic acid.

W

Water Bath

A water container is used to speed up the cooling process of a candle.

Wet Spots

Wet spots represent the wax areas pulled away from containers leaving spots. Wet spots are a common issue for container candles and are also referred to as delamination.

Wick

The medium that distributes fuel to the flame in a candle.

Wick Bar

A tiny metal piece that is used to stabilize the wick at the surface of a candle.

Wick Clip Assembly

This is a precut wick length with a wick tab earlier crimped in place.

Wick Down

Using a wick that is one size smaller but within the identical series.

Wick Up

To use a wick one size bigger and part of the same series. For example: going from an LX-24 to an LX-26.

Wick Pin

The wick pin is replacing the wick while pouring pillar or votive candles. This item is then removed once the candle has cooled off evenly and a wick is fixed in its central place.

Wick Tab

The wick tab is a flat metal disc containing a tiny hole in the middle for a wick. The Wick tab keeps the wick at the base of the candle.

Conclusion

S o, this happened. We are at the end of a road. And what a journey it had been. I do hope that after reading this book, you are one step closer to fulfilling your dream and more are confident that you have what it takes to step out of your comfort zone and make a name for yourself. Of course, I also hope that you don't hate me for getting into some not very pleasant notions to read. You know that I did it only to prepare you for what's out there.

Anyway, not when only a few more words stand between you and your dream. I want to thank you for supporting me as much as you did, and I want to thank you for the trust you've shown me. Because

I never claimed to be an expert, I only claimed to be a person who started right from where you are standing and who made it simply because she was too desperate and stubborn to quit. Thus, once again, I bow before you and thank you.

But before we say our goodbyes, I want us to review for the last time everything we've discussed here.

So we've talked about the history of candles and understood their importance and how they got to become what they are today. Correct?

After that, we moved to the reasons why it's a good idea to start a candle-crafting business. But we've understood the challenges and the downsides of this idea.

We then moved to a somehow boring but extremely necessary part about everything you need to know for starting a company, only to jump to the beauty of crafting and understanding the importance of each raw material. We talked about the types of candles, how to manufacture your products, and also ship them, making sure that they arrive safe and sound at their final users.

Last but not least, we moved to another tricky topic which is marketing, a topic that I hope from the bottom of my heart that you understood.

This being said, yes, it has been a hell of a rollercoaster, but we made it, and we did it together. So, let me congratulate you and wish you the best of luck in the times to come.

The last piece of advice? Don't wait for too long before you make your dreams come true. We only live once, and life is simply too short not to take chances.

Your Opinion Matters

First of all, thank you for purchasing this book. I know you could have picked any number of books to read, but you picked this book, and I am incredibly grateful for that. If you enjoyed this book and found some benefit in reading this, I'd like to hear from you and hope that you could take some time to post a review on Amazon. Your feedback and support will mean a lot to me and will help me significantly for future projects.

Thanks!

Customer Reviews

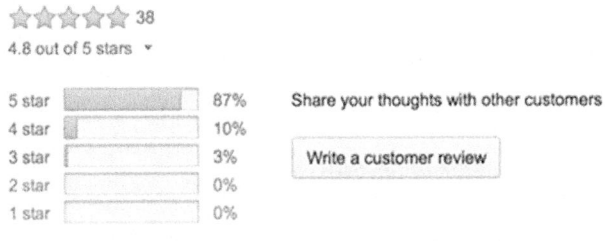

4.8 out of 5 stars ▾

5 star		87%
4 star		10%
3 star		3%
2 star		0%
1 star		0%

See all 38 customer reviews ›

Share your thoughts with other customers

Write a customer review

Printed in Great Britain
by Amazon

25726977R00106